ON THE ROAD
WITH JESUS

BEN WITHERINGTON III

ON THE ROAD WITH JESUS

BIRTH AND MINISTRY

Abingdon Press
Nashville

Library of Congress Cataloging-in-Publication Data

Witherington, Ben, 1951–
    On the road with Jesus : birth and ministry / Ben Witherington III.
        p.   cm.
    ISBN 978-1-4267-1215-9 (trade pbk. : alk. paper)
    1. Jesus Christ—Biography.   2. Bible. N.T. Gospels—Criticism, interpretation, etc.
I. Title.
    BT301.3.W54   2011
    232.9′01—dc22

                                                                        2011015034

11 12 13 14 15 16 17 18 19 20—10 9 8 7 6 5 4 3 2 1

MANUFACTURED IN THE UNITED STATES OF AMERICA

Whoever he was or was not, whoever he thought he was, whoever he has become in our memories since and will go on becoming for as long as we remember him—exalted, sentimentalized, debunked, made and remade to the measure of each generation's desire, dread, indifference—he was a man once, whatever else he may have been. And he had a man's face, a human face.

Ecce homo, Pilate said—*Behold the man*—yet we tend to shrink back from trying and try instead to behold Shakespeare's face or Helen of Troy's, because with them the chances are we could survive almost anything. . . . But with Jesus the risk is too great; the risk that his face would be too much for us if not enough, either a face like any other to see, pass by, forget, or a face so unlike any other that we would have no choice but to remember it always and follow or flee it to the end of our days and beyond. . . .

Nobody tells us what he looked like, yet of course the New Testament is what he looked like, and we read his face in the faces of all the ones he touched. . . . Take it or leave it, the face of Jesus is, if nothing else, a face we would know anywhere . . . a face we somehow belong to. Like the faces of the people we love, it has become so familiar that unless we take pains we hardly see it at all. Take pains. See it for what it is . . . see it too for what it is just possible that it will become: the face of Jesus as the face of our own . . . innermost destiny.

—Frederick Buechner

CONTENTS

PREFACE

It is an interesting fact that of all the figures in the New Testament, indeed of all the figures in the Bible, only Jesus calls people to come and follow him—as it were, to set themselves in motion with him. We are all familiar with the dictum of Jesus: "If anyone would come after me, let him take up his cross and follow me" (Matthew 16:24, paraphrased). Following, it would appear, was not the same as being a disciple of some Jewish sage or teacher or rabbi. Being a student entailed going and sitting in the dust at the feet of the Jewish teacher and learning from him. It involved sitting still and listening. It also involved imitating the teacher's ways, manners, and behaviors. It did not involve simply "following" him around, although, to be sure, Jesus had a "following." Consider for a moment Luke 8:1-3:

> Soon after this, Jesus was going through towns and villages, telling the good news about God's kingdom. His twelve apostles were with him, and so were some women who had been healed of evil spirits and all sorts of diseases. One of the women was Mary Magdalene, who once had seven demons in her. Joanna, Susanna, and many others had also used what they owned to help Jesus and his disciples. Joanna's husband, Chuza, was one of Herod's officials. (CEV)

Jesus is on the road again, and he has both male and female followers, and ultimately this will lead them to Jerusalem, lead them to a cross, and lead them to a crossroads in their own lives. "They will have to follow or flee Him for all the rest of their days," as Frederick Buechner puts it. Jesus is completely clear from the outset that it can end with them giving the last full measure of their devotion—death on a cross. "Take up your cross, and follow me," says Jesus.

Following is far more than merely learning from, admiring, and imitating; it is setting your life in motion in such a way that in some sense the pattern of your life takes on the pattern of Jesus' life. His story becomes not merely history, but your story. This is where the story is tending and intending to go. But to understand that ending, we must start back at the beginning. In this first study of Jesus, we will be walking through and working through the story from before the angel's appearance to Mary, the Annunciation, to the announcement, when Jesus first made his intentions for his ministry plain from the synagogue, both of which take place in Nazareth. We will be following the story from Nazareth to Bethlehem to the Jordan to the Judean wilderness to Capernaum and the Sea of Galilee to Cana and back to Nazareth. Here is your invitation not merely to come and follow this text or the story it tells, though you must do that, but to come and follow, learn, and finally, become like him.

CHAPTER ONE

UNTO US A SON IS GIVEN

*All the Gospels present Jesus on a continual road trip—
God in motion, urgently making a way to us in defeat of
the desert in which we wander. —William H. Willimon*

MARY, MARY—EXTRAORDINARY

It is possible to begin the story of Jesus from before time and
space, to begin it like a *Star Wars* introduction with "the story
thus far" scrolling through the galaxy, bringing us up-to-date. In
fact, this is where John 1 begins the story. You can almost hear
James Earl Jones in his deep baritone saying not "long, long ago
in a galaxy far, far away" but even more impressively, echoing
Genesis 1: "In the beginning was the Word, and the Word was
with God, and the Word was God. He was in the beginning with
God." Scholars call this the preexistence language applied to
God the Son, speaking about where he was and who he was and
what he was doing before there ever was a material universe,
before there was ever the proclamation "Let there be light."

This way of starting the story is breathtaking and challenging.
This is the language of "Incarnation," of how the preexistent,
divine Son of God took on flesh and dwelt among us. Indeed, the

very term *Incarnation* implies that the person in question existed before he became a human being. The poet John Donne, reflecting on this very matter, wrote in his holy sonnet, which begins with the words "Wilt thou love God, as he thee? Then digest": " 'Twas much that man was made like God before, / But, that God should be made like man, much more." Indeed. It's one thing to talk about human creatures being created in the image of God and something different altogether to talk about God taking on the image of human beings. And one has to be exceedingly careful about how one talks about this matter.

For example, I like to ask my New Testament students, "Did Jesus always exist?" Some of them, without hesitation, will say, "Of course, John 1 and Philippians 2:5-11 make this clear." Then I will reply, "I did not ask, did the divine Son of God always exist? I asked, did Jesus, the human being, always exist?" Some of the brighter sparks in the class then get the point. Jesus is the name of a human being. If the Incarnation is real, if the Word really did, at some particular point in time, take on flesh, then the story of Jesus has a temporal beginning. There is a point in time when this person is given a human name because he has a temporal human beginning. Strictly speaking, before the Incarnation, before the virginal conception, there was no Jesus the human being. There was only the divine Son of God who "became" Jesus when he took "on flesh." And here is the great mystery—*he did this without leaving behind his divine nature.* The Word took on flesh in an additive process. The Word did not cease to be the divine Son of God when he did so. But the story of Jesus, properly speaking, begins with the story of Mary. It begins with an announcement and a human response by Mary that has momentous, indeed everlasting, consequences. As it turns out, from the outset, mere mortals become part of the story, part of the plan of God to save our world.

We owe the story of the Annunciation to Luke. We have heard it so many times that we are probably inoculated against really hearing it. It is a story about the unexpected, the dangerous, the improbable, the surprising. Let us hear the tale again and try to listen with new ears and an open mind.

2

When Elizabeth was six months pregnant, God sent the angel Gabriel to Nazareth, a city in Galilee, to a virgin who was engaged to a man named Joseph, a descendant of David's house. The virgin's name was Mary. When the angel came to her, he said, "Rejoice, favored one! The Lord is with you!" She was confused by these words and wondered what kind of greeting this might be. The angel said, "Don't be afraid, Mary. God is honoring you. Look! You will conceive and give birth to a son, and you will name him Jesus. He will be great and he will be called the Son of the Most High. The Lord God will give him the throne of David his father. He will reign over Jacob's house forever, and there will be no end to his kingdom."

Then Mary said to the angel, "How will this happen since I haven't had sexual relations with a man?"

The angel replied, "The Holy Spirit will come over you and the power of the Most High will overshadow you. Therefore, the one who is to be born will be holy. He will be called God's Son. Look, even in her old age, your relative Elizabeth has conceived a son. This woman who was labeled 'unable to conceive' is now six months pregnant. Nothing is impossible for God."

Then Mary said, "I am the Lord's servant. Let it be with me just as you have said." Then the angel left her. (Luke 1:26-38 CEB)

Mary is a small-town girl, a mere teenager, probably a young teenager, engaged to be married and minding her own business when she receives a visit from one of God's FedEx boys, God's special messengers. And it's not just any angel sent to deliver the news, but Gabriel, one of the two great angels, who, along with Michael, was involved with and watched over God's people, Israel. Mary, whose name is in fact Miryam, named after the sister of Moses, the famous Old Testament prophetess, is of course dumbfounded by what the angel says. But why? Hadn't she read Isaiah or at least heard from the scroll of Isaiah taught in the Nazareth synagogue?

The answer to this question may surprise you. Isaiah 7:14 reads in the Hebrew: "And a young nubile woman of marriageable age will conceive and give birth to a child." Yes, this verse implies that the woman would be a virgin. This text was written in an honor-and-shame culture where the virginity of the bride was of paramount importance and taken for granted. However, this text does not focus specifically on the virginity of the woman, though the later Greek (LXX) translation of this verse does more narrowly stress the virginity of the woman in question. That LXX text is what Matthew quotes in his treatment of the story. But even if the Hebrew text was taken to read, "And a virgin will conceive and give birth to a child," the normal and natural assumption would be that she would conceive by normal means, which is to say, with benefit of a husband. The text does not explain *how* the woman would come to be pregnant. Thus it was that the notion of a virginal conception would come as more than a little surprising to a young Jewish girl like Mary. No one in her context was likely thinking that the Jewish Messiah would come into this world through miraculous means. After all, King David and King Solomon had come into this world like everyone else—through the efforts of their parents. They did not come into this world trailing clouds of glory.

Let me be clear that Isaiah 7:14 can be interpreted to refer to a virginal conception. It's just not so specific that it rules out other ways of reading this piece of prophetic poetry. And clearly, Jews of Mary's time did read it differently. What prompted the followers of Jesus to read this story in a very specific way was the event that happened in the life of Mary—an unexpected, unlooked-for event—a virginal conception. The event caused the rereading of Scripture in a fresh way. You will notice that I did not call this miracle "the virgin birth." The miracle in this case transpires at the point of conception, not at the point of the birth of Jesus, which from all we can tell took place in a normal manner. And we might well ask: why the need for a virginal conception? After all, Joseph was a good, God-fearing man; there is nothing unclean or unholy about human sexual intercourse between a husband and wife in and of itself.

The answer to this question has to do with the darkness into which the light of the world came. Remember what John 1:5

says: "The light shines in the darkness, and the darkness did not overcome it." Jesus was born into a dark, dangerous, sinful world. He was born into a world where people loved darkness more than light. In short, he was born into a fallen world, a world that C. S. Lewis once aptly characterized as a place where it was "always winter and never Christmas." The world was in a sorry state; it was lost. And more to the point, human beings had fallen into sin and degradation and could not get up on the basis of their own efforts or understanding or willpower. Salvation would have to come in the form of a radical rescue effort, not a human self-help program. It would come to do its work "as far as the curse is found." The virginal conception tells us that the savior would have to come into the world and be truly human without being a sinner, without having a fallen human nature. Only so could the Messiah be the literal Holy One of God; only so could he be the unblemished Lamb of God who takes away, rather than adds to, the sins of the world. As the author of the book of Hebrews was later to say, Jesus was tempted like us in every respect, save without sin. The virginal conception reminds us it would take a miracle to sort out the human dilemma and save humanity from itself.

What does it mean for Jesus to be truly human? Though some people through the ages have equated being human with being a sinner, the writers of the New Testament are not among them. To be truly human means to live in human form and live with the normal limitations humans have—limitations of time and space and knowledge and power. It means to live with the limitation of mortality. God, however, never intended for sin to be an inherent or built-in component of what it means to be human. As Alexander Pope once said, "To err is human"; but the reverse of that is not true—one must err, one must sin, to be truly human. Jesus was truly human and yet not a sinner. He was Adam gone right, or, as Paul was later to call him, the last Adam, the last and true founder of the human race. I suspect that some of these ideas help explain why Jesus chose to call himself the "Son of Man." We will say more about these things when we discuss Jesus' temptations in the wilderness, but we must return to the Annunciation, the announcement to Mary.

Let's talk for a moment about *where* this announcement took place. It took place in a little backwater town, a little one-stoplight town on no major road, called Nazareth. There are no prophecies in the Old Testament alerting the hearer to watch out for the first announcement of the coming of the Messiah in such a locale. But the name of the town is something of a clue. Literally it is "Netzer-it," meaning Branch Town, which is an allusion to the fact that a shoot or branch will come forth from Jesse and will be the final and greatest descendant of the line of David—the final, true Son of David, who will save his people. It appears that the town of Nazareth was a place to which descendants of David moved. This helps explain why it is that when the census rolls around (see Luke 2:1-3), Mary and Joseph have to go back to the ancestral town to register. Some of those families who had come from Bethlehem had ended up in Nazareth and now had to go back to the old home place for the registration. This is a tale of two cities, but quite unlike Charles Dickens's tale of London and Paris. Instead, this is a tale of two small Jewish villages where the history of the world was to be irrevocably altered.

The second thing to notice about this story is that Mary is betrothed. When we think of betrothal, we may not think of a formal and binding contract, but in the world of Mary, betrothal is a formal and legal commitment, and the only way to get out of it is to break the contract, indeed to divorce the person. This is why Matthew's account of this story at one point says that when Joseph found out his wife was pregnant, knowing he was not the father, he resolved to divorce her quietly; though, honestly, how it could be kept quiet in a tiny village like Nazareth is a good question. The situation of Mary would be perilous if she was found to be pregnant out of wedlock and yet was betrothed. Indeed, the possible penalty for such a state was stoning. The story of the virginal conception is a dangerous story, dangerous to its principal character—Mary. Mary would be taking an enormous risk not merely of being rejected by Joseph, but also of being condemned and stoned, or at least cast out of her village once the story got out about her pregnancy.

Can you imagine the conversation that must have transpired between Mary and her parents after the angelic visitation? "Guess what, Mom and Dad?" says Mary, "I'm going to be the mother of the Messiah." "There, there, dear," says Mary's mother, "every Jewish girl dreams of being the mother of the Messiah." "No, seriously," says Mary, "I am going to be the mother of the Messiah." "And how do you know this?" asks Mary's father. Mary replies, "An angel named Gabriel came and told me, and in fact I am already pregnant with the Messiah; but not to worry, this was a miracle performed by the Holy Spirit. No man has touched me yet." What would you say in these circumstances if your thirteen-or-fourteen-year-old daughter told you a story like this? Would you not think that this might be a cover-up for premarital sex with someone? And indeed, we know that later non-Christian Jewish traditions critical of this very story suggested that Jesus was illegitimate. In fact one version told by Celsus, the Jewish dialogue partner of Origen, was that a Roman soldier named Pantera had impregnated Mary.

You can see immediately how the skeptical would jump to such a conclusion. And this is precisely why it is unlikely that this story in Luke 2 is a mere fable. The earliest Christians, including Luke himself, were attempting to put their best foot forward in regard to the story of Jesus, doing apologetics and evangelizing one and all, and they intended to make clear that Jesus' story was good (and godly) news, not news only fit for soap operas. My point is simple: they would not make up a story about a virginal conception. Furthermore, this story has no precedent. Not even the emperors, who in this era were sometimes called divine or the son of some deity, were thought to have come into the world by means of a virginal conception. This story is without parallel, and its potential to be seen as scandalous by Jews and Gentiles alike, makes it unlikely to have been invented by the Evangelists. Furthermore, Matthew and Luke, in two otherwise very different accounts, are in agreement, probably independently of each other, that the virginal conception definitely happened.

In 1978, when my wife and I were living in England, I had the task of teaching a children's Sunday school class at our local Methodist church in Durham. It was the Christmas season and I had been telling the children the story of the Annunciation and the virginal conception. One young lady named Rachel, who was very bright and about seven or eight, came up to me after class and asked the following excellent question, "Now, let me see if I have got this right. If God is Jesus' father, and Mary is Jesus' mother, are God and Mary married?" This was followed by a dramatic pause, and then in a softer voice, "And if not, is Jesus illegitimate?" Out of the mouths of babes. Rachel had rightly sensed the potentially scandalous nature of this story if Mary's pregnancy was not miraculous, as the story claims. I explained to Rachel that God and Mary were not married—indeed she would go on to marry Joseph and have more children, the brothers and sisters of Jesus—but that God through the Holy Spirit had given Mary the gift of a child: "Unto us a son is given."

Next, let's look at the reassurance the angel gave Mary. He told her not to worry, for the Lord was with her, by which I assume he meant that God was looking after her and that she had the singular honor of being chosen by God, of being highly favored by God, to bear the Messiah, who, as Luke says, would be the savior of the world. Notice as well that neither Mary nor Joseph get to choose the name of this child. The angel says that he shall be called Jesus, which is to say Yeshua, much the same as the name Joshua, which means "Yahweh saves." What an appropriate name for the Messiah. The promise says that this child will be called Son of the Most High God, will be given a throne, and will rule over Israel forever.

Now, if you are reading this story in its appropriate context, namely in light of Luke 1, you will notice there is a contrast between this story and the story of what happened to Zechariah when he received his visitation. Mary's response to the angel is simply, "How will this happen since I haven't had sexual relations with a man?" (v. 34 CEB). This is unlike Zechariah's query, "How will I know that this is so?" (v. 18). Mary is simply asking the *means* by which this is to happen. Zechariah appears to be asking a doubting question, asking for proof, as it were, that what the angel says is true. The former question comes from a posture of faith seeking understanding; the latter from a posture of doubt seeking proof. This is why Zechariah is struck dumb whereas Mary is enabled to praise God and offer us one of the truest and most noble and self-sacrificial statements ever made by a person of faith.

One of the major themes in Luke's Gospel is the theme of reversal—the least, the last, and the lost will become the foremost, the first, and the found. What we have in Luke 1–2 is male-female reversal, with Mary being portrayed as more of a person of deep faith and trust in God than even the priest Zechariah when he is in the Holy of Holies. There is then deep irony when Mary says exactly what Zechariah should have said, "I am the Lord's servant. Let it be with me just as you have said" (Luke 1:38 CEB). In a Gospel full of portrayals of disciples—both female and male disciples—Mary is presented as the first person to respond fully positively to the good news about Jesus, the Messiah, the Savior, the Son of God. As we shall see, however, what happens in Nazareth does not stay in Nazareth. Soon thereafter there is a necessary journey to Bethlehem, where the Messiah is meant to be born, according to the prophecies of Micah 5:2-5.

BORN IN A BARN?

I was in Bethlehem not long ago, in my favorite olivewood shop—The Three Arches. In this shop there was every imaginable size and shape carving of the "Nativity scene." There were even three-foot-tall statues of Mary and Joseph and camels and donkeys. I don't think those will fit in anyone's luggage. One of the interesting things one can study is the history of the celebration of Christmas. For example, did you know that the first person to set up a Nativity scene, in this case a living one, was Saint Francis of Assisi? He's the one who positioned sheep and donkeys and camels together in a single scene, which is hardly a surprise

9

considering his great love for animals. (See the hymn "All Creatures of our God and King.") Unfortunately, sometimes when traditions get going, they are very hard to change. But this tradition is in need of some changing, because, in fact, Luke 2:7 does not say that Jesus was born in a barn. It says that he was laid in a manger, a corncrib, because there was no room in the *katalyma*. What is a *katalyma*? As it turns out, this is the word Luke uses for a guest room. For example, in Luke 22:11 Jesus asks his disciples to go and requisition a "guest room," a *katalyma*, so that he and the disciples might share the Passover meal. Luke does not use this word to refer to an inn. Luke instead uses the word *pandoxion* for an inn (see, for example, Luke 10:11). The story Luke is telling in chapter 2 about the visit to Bethlehem is not a story about the Holy Family finding no room in the inn and so having to settle for birthing their child in a barn. To the contrary, this is a story about finding no room in the guest room of the ancestral home, and so instead they are put in the space in the back of the house where one normally kept one's beast of burden, hence the corncrib or manager. All of these sermons about Jesus being cast out by the world are not well grounded in Luke's story.

What is well grounded in Luke's story is the fact that we hear that shepherds, generally considered unclean but existing in plentiful quantities in Bethlehem (the center of sheep rearing for the sacrifices in the Temple in nearby Jerusalem, six miles away), themselves receive an angelic message and go to see the birth of their Messiah. Here again the theme of reversal is in play. In Luke there are no visits from kings or their courtiers, the wise men or magi. There is instead a visit from the lowly sheepherders. Jesus really is the savior for everyone up and down the social scale. What this story, of course, also suggests is the humble origins of Jesus and the ordinary nature of his family. They are not patricians; they are not of a priestly line (unlike John the Baptizer); they are not landed gentry like many Sadducees. They are a family of artisans—carpenters or stonemasons or both—for this is what the Greek suggests. This does not make them peasants or illiterate or landless, but it does mean that they are not wealthy.

This impression is only further confirmed by a text like Luke 2:22-24, where we hear that in the process of going through the ritual of purification (something Mary would not likely have done if she felt she was not unclean or not sinful) Mary and Joseph make an offering of two turtle doves and two pigeons. This is not the offering of a wealthy family.

There has been some unnecessary quibbling over the notion that people went to their ancestral homes for tax registration. In fact, this was a historical practice in the early decades of the Roman Empire, as there are records of it in Egypt, the next province over from Judea. There has also been some unnecessary questioning of Luke's knowledge about the census of Quirinius. It is certainly true that there was a famous census by Quirinius in the first decade or so after Jesus' birth, and in fact Luke's text can be read as follows: "This registration happened first, [before] the governorship of Quirinius in Syria." Luke is a careful ancient historian, striving hard to get his facts straight, and in Luke 2 he is syncing up the macrohistory of the empire with the microhistory of Jesus. The irony is, of course, that Jesus was to become much bigger than the empire. The empire would strike out, but Jesus is still going strong.

In regard to the date of Jesus' birth, we can now say with considerable assurance that Jesus was born somewhere between 2 and 6 B.C. Jesus was born before the death of Herod the Great, who died about 2 B.C. Why then is our calendar messed up, such that Jesus was born B.C.—"before Christ"? Well, the answer comes from a medieval monk named Dionysius the Short, or, as some call him, "Denny the Dwarf." Dionysius is the one who did the calculations about when the Christian era began, and he missed it "by that much." He was off anywhere from two to six years. At the other end of the story of Jesus, we can be a bit more precise as to when Jesus died. He died either in early April A.D. 30 (more likely) or in the spring of A.D. 33 (less likely). As Luke himself tells us, he lived only into his early thirties (see Luke 3:23).

STARGAZERS AND CHRISTMAS GIFTS

If we turn back to the manger scene for a moment and compare Luke 2 to Matthew 2, we will discover that it appears the Magi came to visit Jesus and the Holy Family when they were "at home," as the text says. The Magi entered "the house" (Matt 2:11, not the barn) and visited with them, giving them gifts of gold, frankincense, and myrrh. These "Magi" were not present at the birth of Jesus but came sometime afterward. Our crèche or manger scenes reflect Saint Francis's blending of these various stories into a single tale on a single occasion, but the Gospels tell us otherwise.

The Magi, from *magos* (*magi*: the word from which we get the word "magician"), are not kings, nor does the story in Matthew tell us there were three—this is simply a guess based on the number of gifts. Two Magi could have brought three gifts, and so could three or more. We simply do not know. What we do know is that these men were stargazers, astrologers, and they followed a star to Jerusalem and then on to Bethlehem. The behavior reported of the star in Matthew 2:9 (cf. 2:2) is peculiar, and this may reflect the ancient belief that the stars, or at least some of them, were the heavenly host, namely angels, who indeed could guide a person or group of persons to the precise house where the Holy Family was staying. As for their gifts, they are gifts fit for a king, with myrrh perhaps the most interesting of the gifts, since it was used in burials, including royal burials (see John 20).

The story in Matthew 2, like the story in Luke 2, is full of irony. The real king lives humbly; the false king lives opulently. The false king sends the Magi to find (and worship) the real king, but the false king wishes to do him harm. So we have the altogether believable tale of Herod slaughtering the innocents in Bethlehem to protect his throne. Coming from a man who was so paranoid he killed some of his wives as well as some of his offspring, the killing of a few infants in Bethlehem would not be a surprising act. We must remember that Bethlehem, like Nazareth, was a tiny town on no major road, and the population in Jesus' day was minuscule. In fact, there probably wasn't even an inn in Bethlehem, in that era, so small was the village. We should not imagine then a mass execution of dozens of children, when perhaps a half dozen or so were involved. This would have been a minor event in the annals of a king who killed so many to gain and maintain power.

If we are wondering why it is that there is so much focus on where Jesus comes from, it is because in antiquity it was often believed that geography, generation, and gender determined who you were and could be—and who you weren't and could never be. Perhaps you will remember the conversation in John 1 when one potential follower of Jesus says to another, "We have found the one about whom Moses and the prophets wrote, Jesus, son of Joseph from Nazareth," to which Nathanael rebuts: "Can anything good come out of Nazareth?" (author's translation). In antiquity, cities had honor ratings, and Nazareth was by no means at the top of the list. There was no Jewish expectation of a messiah coming from Nazareth (see John 7:41-42). Notice as well the ironic note that Philip seems to think he knows that Jesus is the son of Joseph. But, in fact, in this Gospel we have already been told that Jesus is the Word who came from God. Jesus' human origins would continue to be controversial throughout his life.

Though it may seem strange to us, ancient people believed that one's personality and character were determined from birth, and thus to some degree so was one's human potential. To be the Messiah you had to be born a Jewish male, you had to come from Bethlehem, and you had to be of the line of David, according to the conventional thinking based on reflection on the Old Testament prophets. Jesus didn't seem to fit the bill. But in fact he had been born in Bethlehem, as both Matthew and Luke confirm, though his parents were from and he grew up in Nazareth, not Bethlehem. Jesus, in any case, did not come to meet people's expectations of what the Messiah must look like. He came to meet their needs. But there is much more to the story of Jesus than the story of his origins. One also needs to know a good deal about one of his relatives—John, the son of Zechariah and

Elizabeth, a child born out of due season in life, when his parents were old and beyond normal childbearing age.

ENTER JOHN THE ESCHATOLOGICAL PROPHET

It is a fact that all four of the Gospels feel compelled for one reason or another to tell us something of the story of John the Baptizer *at the beginning or even before* the story of Jesus. No one would guess that Luke's Gospel was the story of Jesus, if one read only the first few columns of the original manuscript. Unlike Mark's Gospel (Mark 1:1), Luke does not mention Jesus at the beginning; indeed, he is not mentioned until Luke 1:26-38, where we have the story of the Annunciation. Why exactly was John's story so important to understanding Jesus' story, and what should we make of John?

It is clear that in the Gospels, John will be portrayed as the forerunner of Jesus, and indeed one who will ultimately defer to Jesus, but it would be a mistake to think that John and his movement simply disappeared into the Judean desert once Jesus showed up. In fact, his movement continued on for some decades after his premature death. We hear about followers of John the Baptizer as late as Acts 18 and 19 and in places like Ephesus, a long way from the Judean wilderness. And then there is also the fact that Jesus highly praised John on several occasions, even calling him the greatest person ever born of woman! We would do well then to explore in some depth John and his movement.

In the first place, there is the issue of John and his relationship to the Qumran, or Dead Sea, community. The Qumran community had been in existence for well over one hundred years before John came on the scene as an adult. This community seems to have had a falling out with the Temple hierarchy in Jerusalem, and some priests and others who had purity concerns seem to have gone off into the desert with a leader called the Teacher of Righteousness (we don't actually know who he was) well before the birth of Jesus. They set up their community by the Dead Sea, practiced daily ritual purification rites, ate communally, copied Scripture scrolls and community documents, and awaited the eschatological intervention of God, who would come to judge the corrupt Temple and leadership in Israel. Like John and like Jesus they believed they were living on the cusp of the end times.[1] It is probable that they are the same group whom the first-century Jewish historian Josephus calls the Essenes.

So what is this group's connection with John? The answer involves several things. Notice how in Mark 1 we have the citation of an important scripture from Isaiah 40:3: "A voice cries out: / 'In the wilderness prepare the way of the LORD, / make straight in the desert a highway for our God.'" You will notice how I have punctuated this verse. The verse could also be read "the voice of one crying in the wilderness," where it is the voice in the wilderness rather than the preparation in the wilderness that is stressed. In either case, the wilderness in question, so far as John or the Qumranites were concerned, is the same—the Judean chalk wilderness. The idea is for them to prepare the way for God's coming judgment. It would appear that the theme Scripture that the Qumranites used to justify where they were and what they were doing is also the theme Scripture in the Gospels used to explain John the Baptizer.

Second, both John and the Qumranites were famous for water rituals and some kinds of asceticism. Third, it was God's direct intervention in judgment on Israel's leadership that was to be a core message for both John and the Qumran community. Yes, both John and the Essenes talked about messianic figures coming, but they believed that God's judgment would fall on Israel prior to that or as a part of that whole eschatological scenario. It is my view that John had been a part of this Qumran community but split off and began his own baptismal practice at the Jordan, warning of God's coming wrath. There will be a difference in emphasis between Jesus and John in this regard.

Whereas John emphasizes the coming judgment, Jesus stresses the good news of God's in-breaking, divine, saving activity, or royal reign. Whereas John practices asceticism, Jesus banquets with the bad and even with tax collectors. Whereas John is best known for his baptism of repentance, Jesus himself water-baptized no one during his ministry (though apparently his early disciples, perhaps those who had first been John's disciples, did baptize; see John 4:1-2). The similarities between John and the Qumran community seem stronger than those between John and Jesus. It is perhaps not a surprise then, since Jesus did not seem to be doing the same thing as John, that near the end of John's life he sent some disciples to ask Jesus if he was indeed "the one who is to come, or shall we look for another?" (Matt 11:3; Luke 7:19 ESV). Jesus was carving out his own messianic niche rather than conforming to preconceived notions, even those of John the Baptizer. Why in the world then did Jesus submit to John's baptism? We will probe that issue and others in our next chapter.

NOTE

1. See Witherington, *Revelation and the End Times* (Nashville: Abingdon Press, 2010).

CHAPTER TWO

TROUBLING THE WATERS

The Son came up from the water,
the Spirit descended on the Son,
and the Father spoke to the Son.
It was a gathering of the Trinity.
—*The Early Church Fathers*

The Jordan River, even during the winter torrent, is not a huge river. Don't think the Mississippi; don't think the Ohio; don't even think of the Kentucky River. And in the heat of summer there are plenty of places where it might be called the Jordan Creek. It is, however, the only real river in all of Israel that brings fresh water through an otherwise dry and weary land. When they visit southern Judea or places like Jericho, tourists are constantly surprised to see just how dry and barren and frankly desertlike a good deal of the land is. Southern Galilee is an exception, but we need to remember that irrigation is what has turned a good deal of Israel into a beautiful place in modernity.

In ways we can hardly imagine if we live in most places in the United States, water in the Holy Land is the most precious commodity of all. There is "living water," by which is meant flowing or moving water (see John 4); there is still water in a well, like Jacob's well; there is water so far underground that when you visit Megiddo you find this huge tunnel and stairlike structure that was used to get to the spring so the fortified, walled city could have daily water, even when it was under attack. In Megiddo the tunnel goes down below and outside the city wall just to reach the spring, which is still present today.

On top of the semi-arid conditions in most of Israel, there is also the issue of the seasons. Between late May and mid-October there is no rain, or only a trace. This is why you find huge cisterns in which to capture and store water all over the land. But at least at the Jordan there is a regular daily source of water, which flows into and then out of the Sea of Galilee, also known as Kinnert.

John the Baptizer (please don't call him "the Baptist"; he didn't join a Protestant denomination) had a ministry sometime before Jesus even went public. And a successful and controversial ministry it seems to have been. When we catch up with John in John 1 or Matthew 3, John has been very busy, and he has disciples and admirers in addition to the curious who have come to gawk and see what he is up to. Any excuse for some time away from the daily grind and a lot of hard manual labor, you might think. But in fact, John was anything but just a welcome distraction; he was seen as a real danger—a danger to all sorts of authority figures, both political and religious, in the land. Pharisees, Sadducees, scribes, priests, the temple hierarchy, and of course Herod Antipas all saw him as a threat in various ways. Yes, he was a prophet, but he came from a priestly family. His father had served in Herod's temple no less. And John was offering cleansing from sin and its guilt simply by means of a baptism of repentance. What if the populace got the idea that they didn't have to go all the way to Jerusalem and offer a sacrifice in the Temple in order to receive forgiveness for their sins? John's ministry could be seen as almost seditious, which may in turn explain part of the reason Herod Antipas had him incarcerated in the first place.

An account of John the Baptizer is found in all extant manuscripts of the *Jewish Antiquities* (18.5.2) by Flavius Josephus, who lived from about A.D. 37 to the end of the century. Here is what it says:

> Now, some of the Jews thought that the destruction of Herod's army came from God, and that very justly, as a punishment of what he did against John, that was called the Baptist; for Herod killed him, although he was a good man and commanded the Jews to exercise virtue, both as to righteousness towards one another, and piety towards God, and so to come to baptism; for that the washing would be acceptable to him, if they made use of it, not for the purpose of putting away [or the remission] of some sins, but for the purification of the body; supposing still that the soul was thoroughly purified beforehand by righteousness. Now when [many] others came in crowds about him, for they were very greatly moved [or pleased] by hearing his words, Herod, who feared lest the great influence John had over the people might put it into his power and inclination to raise a rebellion, (for they seemed ready to do anything he should advise,) thought it best, by putting him to death, to prevent any mischief he might cause, and not bring himself into difficulties, by sparing a man who might make him repent of it when it would be too late. Accordingly he was sent a prisoner, out of Herod's suspicious temper, to Macherus, the castle . . . and was there put to death. Now the Jews had an opinion that the destruction of this army was sent as a punishment upon Herod, and a mark of God's displeasure to him.

What is most interesting about this passage from Josephus is that he makes a point of denying that John was offering a baptism of repentance for forgiveness of sins; in fact he goes so far as to claim that the baptism was for those who were already right with God! This flatly contradicts the Gospel accounts about John and his baptism, and it must be said that Josephus seems to be guilty of special pleading here, trying to show that John was no political or religious threat to the authorities.

Listen, for example, to the description of John and his words in Matthew 3:4-12:

John wore clothes made of camel's hair, with a leather belt around his waist. He ate locusts and wild honey.

People from Jerusalem, throughout Judea, and all around the Jordan River came to him. As they confessed their sins, he baptized them in the Jordan River. Many Pharisees and Sadducees came to be baptized by John. He said to them, "You children of snakes! Who warned you to escape from the angry judgment that is coming soon? Produce fruit that shows you have changed your hearts and lives. And don't even think about saying to yourselves, 'Abraham is our father.' I tell you that God is able to raise up Abraham's children from these stones. The ax is already at the root of the trees. Therefore, every tree that doesn't produce good fruit will be chopped down and tossed into the fire. I baptize with water those of you who have changed your hearts and lives. The one who is coming after me is stronger than I am. I'm not worthy to carry his sandals. He will baptize you with the Holy Spirit and with fire. The shovel he uses to sift the wheat from the husks is in his hands. He will clean out his threshing area and bring the wheat into his barn. But he will burn the husks with a fire that can't be put out." (CEB)

There are several aspects to this passage that call for comment. First, John's garb and ascetical behavior seems reminiscent of another famous prophet, namely Elijah, and some thought John was the coming of the eschatological Elijah figure referred to in Malachi 4:5 who would come to warn people that the great and terrible Day of God's wrath was on its way. It is even possible or probable that Jesus viewed John that way, for Jesus says in Matthew 11:14 that John is this Elijah figure if the audience is willing to accept the idea (so also Matt 17:10-12). Whereas Jesus seems to have regarded John as the Elijah figure mentioned in Malachi, John himself in John 1:21 denies it and apparently didn't view himself that way.

Second, notice that John sees his own work as preliminary. There will be a greater baptism following his—one by the Spirit and with fire. Ironically, the baptismal accounts about Jesus say he received that baptism by the Spirit immediately after he had received John's water baptism (see below). Third, notice that John has not taken the Dale Carnegie course in how to win friends and (positively) influence people. He calls some in his audience "snake spawn"! Notice as well that John insists that mere Jewish heredity doesn't guarantee God's acceptance. God can raise up children of Abraham from the stones in the Judean wilderness, and they might even be less hardheaded than some of the audience.

One of the more interesting aspects of the passage from Matthew 3, fully quoted above, is that John seems to envision the same thing as Malachi did: after the coming of the Elijah figure, divine judgment would follow directly. We can begin to understand then why John might be confused about Jesus, especially if John wondered if Jesus himself was that eschatological Elijah figure. It will be remembered that John asks the question from prison, "Are you the one who is to come, or shall we look for another?" (Matt 11:3; Luke 7:19 ESV). Jesus, in his typically indirect fashion, tells John's disciples to say to John that the blind are receiving sight and the lame are walking, and that those who are not offended by Jesus and his activities are blessed. What all of this tells us is that John was a very important prophetic figure in early Judaism, feared by the authorities (see Mark 11:27-33) and greatly revered by the people and by Jesus himself, who derived some of his own disciples from John's disciples. But there could have been no greater endorsement of John's ministry than the fact that Jesus was prepared to submit to the baptism of John, perhaps surprisingly. We must look at that "watershed" episode in Jesus' life.

A WATERSHED EVENT IN THE LIFE OF JESUS

Scholars have made much of John's baptism of Jesus, and because the later Christian tradition would not make up a story about Jesus submitting to some other human being's authority, as the baptismal scene could be read to suggest, few dispute that it actually happened. How should we view the baptism of Jesus? Mark 11:27-33 leaves little doubt that Jesus himself saw John's baptism as "from God," divinely inspired and endorsed. This will in part explain why Jesus might have been willing to submit to it.

Unfortunately, except for the account in Matthew 3:14-15, the Gospel accounts do not provide us with a rationale as to why Jesus got himself baptized by John. Jesus says that this is the proper way that "we may fulfill all righteousness." Notice the reference here to "we." Jesus sees both John and himself as actors in a divine plan and play, and each must play his part.

John and Jesus must, by this act, "fulfill all righteousness." Since John's baptism is a baptism of repentance, it might be natural to think that Jesus meant that even he must repent of his sins in preparation for the coming divine intervention. The problem with this is that the "us" in this text, if we read it that way, implies John also needed to repent. The Matthean portrayal of this scene in fact suggests that John felt unworthy to baptize Jesus and thought the reverse should happen—Jesus should baptize John. Perhaps the key to understanding this event lies elsewhere.

Let us consider, first of all, who John intended to call to repentance—namely the people of Israel, whether high or low, well-to-do or ne'er-do-well, pious or impious. Judgment would come and begin with the household of God, not with the Gentiles, and so the people of Israel must be warned to repent first and foremost. God expected more of his people than he did of others, for to whom more is given, more is required. It is then possible that Jesus, by submitting to this baptism, was suggesting that he was doing this as a substitute for Israel, as a sort of proxy baptism. Jesus would take the judgment of God on sin on his own shoulders at the end of his ministry, and here at the beginning of his ministry he showed his willingness to do this—in token and in pledge. Jesus is Adam gone right, but perhaps also Israel gone right, the obedient Son of God. Put another way, Jesus will play the role Israel should have played—of repenting and doing the will of God and being a light to the nations and so on. It is possible this is what Matthew had in mind in his description of why Jesus submitted to John's baptism. Bearing this in mind, let us look in some depth at our earliest portrayal of the baptism of Jesus: Mark 1:9-11.

The first thing we need to know about this miniature portrayal of the event is that Mark portrays this from Jesus' point of view—as almost a private matter. The voice from heaven speaks only to Jesus: "You are my Son," and it is said to be Jesus alone who sees the sky crack and the Spirit descending upon him. In short, Mark is portraying this scene as an example of Jesus receiving a vision from God—an apocalyptic vision that confirms his identity to him and sets him in motion to begin his ministry. One can compare the apocalyptic elements in this story (skies rent asunder, Spirit descending, voice from heaven heard) with the similar account of a vision to John of Patmos in Revelation 1.[1] Something dramatic happened to and for Jesus on this occasion. Prior to the baptism, Jesus had not been engaging in a public ministry; he had not been collecting followers. After the baptism and the temptation of Jesus, all of that changed.

The second thing to notice about this story is that the Gospel writers are unconcerned about various things that might concern us about the story. For example, nothing is said about the mode of baptism here (sprinkling, pouring, immersion—though it may well have been the latter). The Greek verb *baptidzo* in itself does not specify a certain quantity of water. Furthermore, the story itself does not suggest or imply that one receives the Spirit in or with or by means of the act of water baptism. In fact, it says the opposite. It says that it was only when Jesus was coming up out of the water that the Spirit descended on him.

Third, we are not told that this happened to anyone else receiving John's baptism. This means that John's baptism was not the equivalent to later Christian baptism, which according to Matthew 28 is done in the name of Father, Son, and Spirit, and according to Acts could be done simply in the name of Jesus. John did not baptize Jesus in the name of Jesus. John's baptism was not the same as later Christian baptism, nor did it serve the same purpose. John's baptism was intended to prepare Israel for God's coming judgment.

Notice as well that the story says that the Spirit descended on Jesus "like a dove." This is simply an analogy. We are not being told that the Spirit descended in the form of a dove, much less that a literal dove alighted on Jesus' shoulder! Presumably what this means is that the Spirit fell gently on Jesus, enabling him to hear the divine voice—just as was the case of John of Patmos, who was in the Spirit on the Lord's Day when he heard and saw a vision from God. We may contrast this gentle anointing by the Spirit with the Spirit's action immediately after the baptism, where we hear: "And the Spirit immediately drove him out into the wilderness" (Mark 1:12).

The most important aspect of this whole event is what Jesus heard the Father say to him as he was exiting the Jordan: "You are my Son, the Beloved; with you I am well pleased" (Mark 1:11). This is a combination citation involving Psalm 2:7 ("You are my son") and Isaiah 42:1 ("in whom my soul delights") from the Old Testament. What we need to recognize about the context of those two Old Testament passages is that the former is part of a coronation ode where the priest says to the Davidic king that he is now in a special sense God's son (see 2 Sam. 7), and the latter passage is addressed to the servant upon whom God has put his Spirit. And then Isaiah relates that God goes on to say: "I have called you in righteousness, / . . . I have given you as a covenant to the people, / a light to the nations, / to open the eyes that are blind, to bring out the prisoners from the dungeon" (Isa 42:6-7). I suggest that Jesus knew perfectly well the context of these two sayings and would have taken them to mean that God had called him to be the royal or messianic One and that he should view his ministry in light of the description of the servant in Isaiah 40–66. He would fulfill the role that "Israel, my servant" had in fact failed to fulfill thus far. And indeed the alert reader will remember that Jesus himself will cite Isaiah 61:1 and say that that text, which echoes Isaiah 42, will be fulfilled on the day he preaches in Nazareth. We will say much more about this in the last chapter of this study, but consider this a preview of coming attractions.

The baptism of Jesus was a watershed event—quite literally—in Jesus' life; but what immediately followed it comes as something of a surprise. The nefarious one—the devil—will severely tempt Jesus.

ATTEMPTING TO OVERCOME A TEMPTING

C. S. Lewis, in the first book I ever read by him, has a lot to say about the devil. I am referring to the famous book entitled *The Screwtape Letters*. For me, the most profound thing he said in that book was that the devil encourages the doubting of his existence so that he may go on doing his devilish work. The devil uses the smokescreen of human doubt to carry on with his mission undercover. There are of course a lot of sophisticated people who think they are too intelligent to believe in anything as primitive as demons and a devil.

Jesus wasn't one of them. He certainly believed in the reality of a personal supernatural evil one, a fallen angel. Indeed at one point in his ministry the exorcisms had been so successful that Jesus remarked to his disciples, "I watched Satan fall from heaven like a flash of lightning," by which he probably meant he saw himself as overturning the work of the devil through exorcisms, among other things (Luke 10:18). And if Jesus had been asked at some juncture if he "believed in Satan's existence," he would have retorted, "Believe in him? I've encountered him!" The story told in Matthew 4:1-11 and Luke 4:1-13 deserves close scrutiny. Here again, what we seem to be talking about is a real but visionary experience, only this time it's not God that Jesus "envisions," it's Satan.

Early Jews had a rather robust theology about demons and Satan. The name *Satan* comes from the Hebrew *ha satan*, meaning "the adversary," and this appears in Job 1–2 where Satan is envisioned as the prosecuting attorney in the heavenly court, the accuser of the brothers and sisters. We do not have a full-scale story of Satan in Scripture, but we have enough to know some basic things about him; namely, he is a fallen angel (see Rev 20:1-3), and he has underlings who work for him, called "demons" in the Gospels. Satan has various other names or descriptors by which he is labeled. *Ho Diabolos* is one, usually translated "the devil." It is the Greek word from which we get the English term *diabolical*. A phrase Jesus used to describe Satan is "the prince of the power of the air." He is also called Beelzebul, which is a play on words: Baal-zebub means "Baal (the Canaanite storm god) is my prince," but Jews turned that honorific title into a comic one—Beelzebul means "the prince or lord of the flies." Much more could be said along these lines, but we need now to look at the temptation story of Jesus, as we learn much about Jesus from examining it closely.

First we must notice that Jesus can indeed be tempted. He is truly human; and indeed the author of Hebrews will say that he was tempted like us in all respects, save without sin. If Jesus had been incapable of sin, then temptations could never really have been tempting to him, for he could never have been inclined to do evil. It is an interesting fact that the Greek word *peirasmos* can be translated as either "tested" or "tempted." If we are seeking to understand the difference between these two things, one traditional way of putting it is that whereas God will test a person, the devil will tempt him or her. As James, the brother of Jesus, insists in James 1, God tempts no one and is not temptable. The difference between a test and a temptation is that a test is intended to strengthen one's character, whereas a temptation is intended to destroy one's character. I would suggest that the proper way to translate the relevant verses in the Lord's prayer is: "Do not put us to the test, but deliver us from the evil one," for after all this a prayer prayed to God, and God tempts no one.

Jesus experiences a threefold temptation in the Judean wilderness, somewhere near the Jordan. He goes from having a close encounter with God to having a close encounter with Satan, both in the form of visions. I need to stress that the ancients did not see visions as merely subjective phenomena or figments of an overactive human imagination—a sort of movie playing only in the cerebral cortex of someone's head. They believed visions were objective things that came to the spiritually aware and open, sometimes from God, sometimes from some other super-natural being.

Notice that according to Luke, Jesus was tempted for the full forty days he was in the wilderness, and during that time he ate nothing. Matthew may suggest that the temptations primarily happened after the forty days of fasting, or the fasting and temptations could be seen as happening simultaneously in Matthew. In any case, what we know is that fasting in a desert can certainly put a person into a liminal state where he or she can be more open to abnormal and paranormal experiences.

There seems to be a progression in these temptations—a temptation to turn stones into bread, a temptation to throw oneself down from the pinnacle of the Temple, and a temptation to worship Satan as a shortcut to being the ruler of the kingdoms of this world. The temptations increase in intensity or severity and in gravity from least to most. Notice as well that in each case the premise is, "If you are the Son of God . . . ," and Satan assumes Jesus is. Satan, it would appear, knows perfectly well that Jesus is the person that the heavenly vision at the baptism confirmed to Jesus he was: the Son of God.

Now, these temptations of Jesus are no ordinary temptations. I have known people who could turn bread into stones, but I have never met a sane person who was tempted to turn stones into bread, for the very good reason that it is not really a possibility for mere mortals. Furthermore, if I threw myself off the pinnacle of the Temple in Jerusalem, all I would experience is a heavy bit of gravity and a crash landing. Normal human beings don't have such temptations. Finally, though I have met some megalomaniacs in my day, I have never met any normal human being who thought it was really possible that he or she could rule the world merely by worshiping an angel! My point is this: Jesus is not experiencing normal human temptations in this story; he is experiencing only temptations that the divine Son of God might have! And the gist of the matter is that Satan is tempting Jesus to act in a manner that is not really possible for ordinary persons and *doing so would obliterate his true humanity.*

27

What I mean by this is that the nature of the Incarnation is that the Son of God assumed all normal human limitations—limitations of time, space, knowledge, and power. God has no such limitations and cannot be tempted. In this scene, Jesus is being tempted to draw on his divine nature, which he has, in such a fashion that he violates, indeed obliterates, his true humanity. Notice for example what Paul says about the Incarnation in Philippians 2:6: "[The Son of God], though he was in very nature God, did not regard equality with God something to be taken advantage of, but rather stripped/emptied himself, taking the very nature of a servant and being born in human likeness" (author's translation). Again, I would stress, Satan is tempting Jesus to act in a fashion that will violate the limitations he willingly took on in the first place in order to be truly human. Jesus, unlike the rest of us, could have called upon his divine nature, as Satan tempted him to do, but he resisted this temptation.

Instead, Jesus resists the devil by drawing on the same two resources every follower of God has to draw on in a time of temptation—the word of God and the Spirit of God. Notice that Jesus quotes Scripture to the devil—first Deuteronomy 8:3, to which Satan responds by quoting Psalm 91:11-12, which Jesus rebuts by quoting Deuteronomy 6:16. They are having a "verse off," as part of their face-off. Then Jesus responds to the last temptation by citing Deuteronomy 6:13. It can be no accident that the first citation is from the story of the wilderness wanderings of Israel and of Moses reminding the Israelites that God allowed them to be tested in wilderness—to be hungry and then to have heavenly manna to remind them that "one does not live by bread alone, but by every word that comes from the mouth of God." The second quotation comes from a psalm about divine protection in the midst of trial and temptation. But this quotation is not found on the lips of Jesus; rather it comes from the lips of the devil himself. He seeks to fight fire with fire by quoting back to Jesus a scripture that would supposedly justify Jesus attempting what Satan is tempting him to do. Jesus responds by quoting back Scripture, this time Deuteronomy 6:16, which in its original context is a warning to the Hebrews not to put God to the test as they did at Masah. If in the first temptation Jesus responds as if he were one of the Hebrews in the wilderness, in the case of the second temptation Jesus may in fact be suggesting that Satan should not tempt God (in this case God the Son); or perhaps the citation is meant to make us think that Jesus is suggesting that for him to do what Satan asked would be a case of his tempting his own heavenly Father, something Scripture forbids. The text probably means the latter. Finally, Jesus rebuts the last temptation by citing Deuteronomy 6:13, which comes in the context of an affirmation of absolute monotheism. Angels, and perhaps especially fallen ones like Satan, should not be worshiped; only the one, true God should be worshiped.

Jesus had endured and prevailed over the three temptations in the wilderness, temptations only someone who really was the divine Son of God might face, and we are told in the Lukan account that Satan left him "until an opportune time." The temptations of Jesus were not over; they had only taken a hiatus for a while. Of course, the next and last major place we see Jesus enduring temptation is in the Garden of Gethsemane, at the very end of his ministry, so one could say that severe temptations plagued him at the outset and conclusion of his ministry. This leads us to reflect a moment on the humanity, as well as the divinity, of the Christ.

Sometimes the Gospels have been interpreted as if Jesus' human life was just a charade. He just *appeared* to be tempted, since God can't be tempted. He just *appeared* to not know the timing of the Second Coming (see Mark 13:32), but really he knew. He just *appeared* to be unable to do any more miracles in Nazareth because of the unbelief in that place (Mark 6). In fact, this is not the way it was with Jesus. He really did accept the limitations of being truly human. When he performed miracles, he did it by the power of the Spirit; and when he had supernatural or spiritual insight into something someone was thinking, this was something the Spirit revealed to him. And when he was tempted by the devil, he relied on the word of God to resist those temptations, just as any other human being can do.

Sometimes devout Christians make the mistake of thinking Jesus was sort of 90 percent divine and 10 percent human. In fact, as the church fathers were to affirm later at Chalcedon, in the fifth century A.D., Jesus was both fully and truly human and fully and truly divine. And the only way that could happen was by divine condescension—by God coming down and taking on not merely flesh but also the limitations of being truly human. In short, the Incarnation was real, and Jesus lived by and according to its limitations even though he was sorely tempted to push the God button from time to time.

Having passed the test in the desert, it was time to return to Galilee and call disciples, gather a following, and set out on a course of ministry. In our next chapter we will examine the beginnings of that process and that period in Jesus' life.

NOTE

1. See Witherington, *The Gospel of Mark* (Grand Rapids: William B. Eerdmans, 2001) on Mark 1.

CHAPTER THREE

FISHING FOR FOLLOWERS: THE CAST OF CHARACTERS

The use of the phrase fishers of men, *in the Old Testament, always has a negative tone, a tone of judgment (Jer 16:16; Ezek 29:4 ff; Amos 4:2; Hab 1:14-17), but Jesus turns this phrase in a new direction. In Jesus' hands the language is active: they are to become Jesus' companions, yes, but to enter into His mission, not to observe it, to be part of Jesus' work, not just witnesses to it.*

—Larry Hurtado

Jewish teachers did not post want ads in synagogues saying, "Disciples wanted, apply within." So far as we can tell, Jewish teachers accumulated disciples or students by means of building reputations as scholars of the Scriptures and the students then sought them out and studied in their homes or later perhaps in the synagogues. Jesus, however, sought out followers after his baptism and temptations in the wilderness. And he seems to have done this with a great sense of urgency in his tone. His initial message appears to have echoed John's calling for repentance, only Jesus added a new twist to the exhortation "The time is fulfilled and the dominion of God is at hand; repent and believe the good news" (Mark 1:15 author's translation). We need to unpack this initial message, as it will help us understand Jesus' calling for followers.

THE INITIAL SALVO—MARK 1:15

In the first instance, Jesus says that the "time is fulfilled." This is not unlike the language Paul uses about the Incarnation itself: "But when the fullness of time had come, God sent his Son" (Gal 4:4). There is a sense that the right time, the righteous time, God's time for divine intervention and redemption, has arrived, and the one who is bringing it in is Jesus himself. But what does Jesus mean by "the dominion of God"?

You will notice that I am deliberately not translating the Greek word in question as "kingdom." This is because the English word *kingdom* suggests a place, whereas the Semitic term *malkuta* can refer to a reign as well as a realm, a rule as well as a place where the rule happens. If one studies all the references to this term in the Gospels, one quickly realizes that sometimes the term has a more verbal sense (the reigning or ruling of God) and sometimes it has more of a noun sense (the realm of God). If we look even more closely, we discover that when Jesus uses the term in the present tense he is talking about the divine saving activity of God in the present through his own ministry (e.g., "If I by the Spirit of God cast out demons, then you will know the dominion has broken into your midst" [Matt 12:28 author's translation]).

Strikingly, when Jesus speaks of this dominion in the future tense, he talks about entering it, obtaining it, and inheriting it, and the sense seems to be that he is referring to a *place*—one that you can enter, obtain, or inherit. For these reasons I suggest the translation "dominion," because one can have dominion over someone (a verbal sense) or one can enter a dominion (a noun sense). The English translation should reflect the flexibility of the original term. What Jesus is referring to in Mark 1:15 then, is that the divine saving activity, God's eschatological intervening to rescue his people, is happening here and now through Jesus. To say this dominion is near is to say that it is close by, accessible now. The proper response then is repentance, as John had previously said, but notice the final clause. If you are going to become a follower of Jesus, you must believe the *good news*—the good news of God. And in a world full of bad news, and in a country ruled by Rome or its impious client kings, that may be difficult to do.

WAS JESUS A RABBI?

Jesus then, when he goes fishing for followers, is not your typical Jewish sage wanting to help his charges better understand Torah. You will not find Jesus dwelling on long sessions of detailed exegesis or interpretation of Old Testament texts. Nor does Jesus ever use footnotes. By this I mean that we never hear him citing previous Jewish sages in the form "I say on the basis of Rabbi Gamaliel, who had it on the basis of Rabbi Shammai, that . . ." To the contrary, Jesus contrasts his own teaching and authority with those who must cite other authorities to say something important. Jesus says, "You have heard that it was said . . . but I say to you . . ." (see Matt 5).

Jesus has come to set the world on fire; he believes that the End Times—the time of the fulfillment of the prophecies and promises of God—are at hand and that the time for leisurely discussion, debate, or dialogue about the Scriptures has mostly come and gone. It is time for a different sort of discipleship. It is time to canvass one and all, warning them about what is about to transpire—both judgment and redemption are at hand. Jesus is not merely asking his followers to come and learn from him; he is asking them to come and follow him, to emulate his actions, indeed even to take up crosses and follow him to Golgotha.

In fact, in Jesus' day, there were no ordained "rabbis" in the official and later sense. Scholars of early Judaism remind us that Judaism was different before A.D. 70, when the Temple was destroyed. Torah, Temple, and Territory were the three *T*s around which religious life revolved before A.D 70, and synagogues were just beginning to be centers of learning and teaching. It was only after the Jewish wars in the 60s and then the Bar Kokhba revolt in the second century that we begin to have something like later rabbinic Judaism, where Torah becomes the almost exclusive focus of religious attention. By then, Jews were even prohibited from going to some places in Jerusalem, and the city was becoming a pagan city named Aelia Capitolina. The term *rabbi* in Jesus' day did not indicate a particular type of teacher or an educational pedigree; it was just a term of respect meaning "my great one" or "my master" (*rabbouni* in the Aramaic; see John 20). It was a term of respect used for a Jewish sage or teacher especially.

FISHING FOR FOLLOWERS

We do not know exactly when Jesus began recruiting followers, but we do know that this seems to have occurred first on the northwest shore of the Sea of Galilee in places like Capernuam, Migdal, Bethsaida, and Korazin. And not surprisingly, Jesus is recruiting fishermen and others who live by the sea, including even tax or toll collectors and women. Most Jewish teachers would have thought there was indeed something "fishy" about the variety of people Jesus was recruiting as followers. These were not those likely to go study at schools in Jerusalem, not those who would necessarily be seen as pious Jews with great spiritual promise and gifts, and in the case of the women, not those who ought to be disciples of a Jewish teacher at all.

The Lukan portrayal of the calling of Simon bar Jonah is perhaps the fullest portrayal of the calling of any of the disciples. Jesus seems to have cured Simon's mother-in-law in Capernaum of some illness, and thereafter called Simon to come and follow him, leaving his nets largely behind. We need not envision Simon becoming Jesus' follower out of the blue, lured by some sort of spiritual gravity Jesus had. Simon had already seen what Jesus could do to cure his mother-in-law and in gratitude was prepared to allow Jesus to use his boat as a speaking platform to address a crowd in Capernaum that was pressing in on the Master. Apparently Jesus was already drawing crowds (on account of the healings) before he began to call disciples to follow him.

But it wasn't Jesus' teaching or even the healing of the mother-in-law that really got to Simon. It was what happened after Jesus taught from the boat on that occasion. Jesus told Simon to row out deeper into the lake and lower his nets for a catch. We can imagine Simon rolling his eyes, as an experienced fisherman might when someone like Jesus gave advice about fishing, and telling Jesus that they had slaved all night trying for a catch and had ended up with nothing. Why in the world, during the daylight hours, when the fish weren't likely stirring, would there be any better outcome? Nevertheless, with a shrug of a shoulder and a response of, "If you say so, I'll give it a try," Simon let down his nets once more, and suddenly the nets were teeming with fish, so much so that Simon had to call to his fellow fishermen, the Zebedee boys, nearby to come help haul in the huge catch. In fact, the boats became so overloaded with fish that they began to sink! Only then did it dawn on Simon that he was in the presence of the holy, and this led to his instinctive response. Right there in the boat, Simon knelt down, and instead of saying, "I will follow you anywhere, anytime," he said, "Go away from me sir, for I am a sinful man." Simon had caught more than he bargained for—a Master! Jesus then enigmatically responded, "Fear not; you'll not need to worry about that sort of fishing anymore. You'll be fishing for human beings." Luke 5:11 ends this amazing tale with the information that it was at this juncture that Simon and the Zebedees left their nets and everything else behind and followed Jesus. It was actually Jesus who had made a great catch on that day.

One of the interesting aspects of this and subsequent recruiting that Jesus did is that he seems to have recruited in pairs, and half of the Twelve seem to have been brothers—Simon and Andrew, James and John, and possibly James son of Alphaeus and Matthew/Levi. There is also the interesting fact that always listed last among the Twelve are Simon the zealot and Judas Iscariot.

This is interesting because the name Iscariot is probably not a family name or even a place name (though it might mean "of Kerioth"). It probably refers to those Josephus calls the *sicarii*— the dagger men among the zealots. The zealots were revolutionaries. They believed in the violent overthrow of Roman rule in Judea, and they didn't much like the Herods either.

What we know about Matthew is that he was a tax or toll collector, ultimately for the Romans or the Herods. Whereas we can imagine Galilean fishermen constantly complaining about the excessive taxes and the traitorous Jews who collected money for these overlords, the relationship between such a tax collector and the zealots can only be called hatred. Jesus seems to have deliberately recruited a volatile mix of disciples, and one supposes he saw them as a microcosm of those he came to save, including the lost and the bad of Israel. What we do not have is a bunch of pious Jews seeking more spiritual formation! These were men from various walks of life, somewhat rough around the edges. In fact, we could imagine all of them initially protesting to Jesus, "Get away from me, Master, for I am a sinful man." Be that as it may, these men ultimately agreed to follow Jesus; and it all started in Capernaum.

THE PETER PRINCIPLE AND HOME BASE

Capernaum was a small fishing village. Its proper name was Kefer Nahum, the village of the prophet Nahum. It was, however, a different prophet, and indeed one greater than a prophet, namely Jesus himself, who had visited this village on the day Simon had the miraculous catch of fish; and it would appear that Jesus was to make it something of a home base, for he seems to have returned to this village again and again during his ministry. Today you can go and see the house of Peter (or his mother-in-law), underneath the Catholic church at the archaeological site at ancient Capernaum, perhaps the earliest meeting place of Jesus' followers. There is graffiti on the walls of this house and other indications that the house was modified to make it a place of worship after the time of Jesus.

Simon, son of Jonah, is the only one of the Twelve for whom we have somewhat of a complete story. He is one of only two male disciples (the other being the Beloved Disciple) about whom we later hear a considerable amount. There may, as well, be a female disciple about whom we have a "before and after" story as well, if Joanna, the wife of Chuza, turns out to be the Junia mentioned in Romans 16. (For more, see pages 43-44.)

Jesus, it seems, was in the business of giving some of his disciples nicknames. The Zebedees were called the "Boanerges," or "sons of thunder," and Simon was called "Cephas"—"rock," or as we might say, "rocky." Of course the English word *rocky* can have either a positive or a negative connotation, and one wonders if Cephas was a double entendre as well. In the famous saying of Jesus in Matthew 16:18, "You are Cephas, and on this shelf of rocks [the second word, *petra*, in the Greek likely does not refer to a single rock, as *petros* would] I will build my community," we have both a nickname given and a promise made (author's translation). It will be remembered that these words of Jesus were given in response to Simon's declaration that Jesus was the Christ, the Son of the living God. The English name Peter comes from the Greek word *petros*, which means rock, being the Greek equivalent of the Aramaic word *Cephas*. What should we make of this tradition about Simon?

The Gospels are pretty clear that Jesus chose twelve male disciples (perhaps symbolically alluding to the twelve tribes of Israel) to itinerate with him, and within that twelve, there were three who served as a sort of inner circle—Simon, James, and John. Of those three there is only one who regularly speaks for the disciples and represents them in relationship to Jesus—Simon. Whereas the three had such unique experiences as being present when Jesus raised Jairus's daughter and seeing Jesus transfigured, only Simon gets the promise that he, as a confessor of faith in Jesus, and presumably those who likewise stood firm on that christological point, would be the basis of Jesus' community going forward. And in John 21, we hear of Jesus recommissioning Simon to tend and

lead the flock after Simon's threefold denial of Jesus in the court-
yard of Caiphas. Thereafter it is in Acts, 1 Corinthians, and the
Petrine literature that we hear about the further adventures and
work of Peter, who according to later Christian tradition was
indeed to be martyred by crucifixion outside Rome (cf. John
21:18-19, which reflects knowledge of Peter's demise).

Simon seems to have been a mercurial person, a passionate person. We remember him vigorously protesting Jesus' washing of his
feet, or we remember him emphatically denying at the Last Supper
that he would abandon Jesus or deny him and then only hours
later, in the heat of the moment, denying Jesus three times! There
is the Peter who attempts to walk on water, which is a greater act
of faith than any of the other members of the Twelve were prepared
to attempt on that occasion, and there is the Peter who opens his
mouth before he has put his brain fully in gear. Notice the account
of the Transfiguration in Mark 9, where Peter, seeing the vision of
Jesus transfigured in the midst of Moses and Elijah (the great
emblems of the Law and the Prophets), suggests he, James, and
John could set up booths and celebrate and preserve the moment.
About this last suggestion, Mark laconically comments that Peter
had no idea whatsoever what he was saying! According to the
Fourth Gospel, it is also Peter who when asked if he and the
Twelve would abandon Jesus, as some followers were abandoning
Jesus because of his shocking teachings, replied, "Lord, where
would we go? You have the words of everlasting life" (John 6:68
CEB, paraphrased). Peter is the only one of the Twelve whom we
really have a full-orbed picture of in terms of habits and personality. This is because the Gospels are not biographies of the Twelve;
they are (in the case of Matthew, Mark, and John) ancient-style
biographies of Jesus. This means that others are only mentioned
insofar as they have some sort of relationship or interaction with
the central figure—Jesus. They are not mentioned for their own
sake or because there is independent interest in them.

Something should be said briefly here about the Twelve as the
Twelve. It appears to me that Jesus chose the Twelve as his agents
to Israel, his "apostles," or missionaries, to implement his ministry
in Israel. They are not called to *be* Israel, but rather to *free* Israel,

and they will be sent out two by two in part because in Judaism the truth of anything needed to be established by the testimony of two witnesses. It will be noticed that they are authorized to do the very same deeds Jesus did, including healings and exorcisms, and they will convey the same dominion message as well.

The term *apostolos* refers to a "sent out one," from the verb *apostello*, or as we would call the person, a missionary. In fact the Semitic term that lies in the background seems to have a business background—*shaliach*, which refers to an authorized agent of someone. This was a person authorized to speak for and transact business for the one for whom he worked, the one who sent him to do some task. He only had limited authority, and it was an authority derived from his master or owner. In early Judaism there was a saying "A man's agent is as himself," which meant that the agent should be treated like the one who sent him—shown the same respect, given the same hospitality, and so on. This agency concept explains, in part, why Jesus tells his disciples, "Inasmuch as they have done it to you, they have done it to me" (Matthew 25:40, paraphrased). To insult or mistreat a man's agent was to mistreat the man himself, as the agent was an extension and a proxy for the one who sent him.

The Twelve then had a very specific mission to Jews, and in particular to Jews in the Holy Land. At one juncture in Matthew (10:5), Jesus tells them, "Go nowhere among the Gentiles," and he even says he was sent only to the lost sheep of Israel. At another juncture, Jesus promises that the Twelve at the eschaton will sit on twelve thrones, judging the twelve tribes of Israel. The Twelve then are Jesus' representatives to Israel, and this explains one of the greater conundrums of the New Testament. Why do the Twelve seem to largely disappear after Easter?

Consider for a moment the book of Acts, which is hardly properly labeled. This is not the Acts of the Apostles; it is more like the Acts of the Holy Spirit, or perhaps the Acts of Peter and Paul and a few others, but not the Twelve. After Acts 1, where a replacement is found for Judas, who hanged himself, the Twelve vanish into the night. We do not hear of them again as an entity or group. This is because Acts chronicles the mission of the church from

Jerusalem to Rome and increasingly to Gentiles.[1] But the Twelve as a group were not sent to the Gentile world, not even to Gentiles in and around Israel. They were sent to Jews in "eretz Israel"—the land of Israel. Of their efforts after Easter we hear precious little, except for a bit about the work of Peter and John in Jerusalem and nearby Samaria. In the book of Acts, a mission in Galilee disappears almost entirely. Perhaps this is what most of the Twelve concentrated on after Easter, but Luke tells us nothing about it, so absorbed is he in chronicling how the Gospel got to Rome and to the Gentile world in general. Jesus, however, did not just have the Twelve as disciples; he had other disciples as well.

JESUS' FEMALE FOLLOWERS

Sometimes the question gets raised: if Jesus was such an advocate for women and their learning potential, why are there no women among the Twelve? There is a simple answer to this question. Jesus had to deal with Judaism as it was in his day, and the way it was in his day was extremely patriarchal in character. It was a man's world, and the Torah was used to reinforce this fact. The witness of a woman was not considered to have real legal status, though often they would be believed. When women had their monthly period, they were not allowed in the synagogue and could not be counted on to make up the quorum of that synagogue for an official meeting. Neither do we hear about women as agents of Jewish teachers, transacting business for such teachers. The Twelve were sent out as the legal agents in relationship to male-dominated Israel. Their witness at least would be taken seriously and not automatically rejected or stereotyped just because of the gender of the person in question.

If you doubt that there was such a prejudice against women's witness in the world of Jesus, just read about the reaction of the male disciples when the women came running to tell them that the tomb of Jesus was empty and that they had seen angels. Luke 24:11 is curt and to the point: "But these words seemed to them an idle tale, and they did not believe them." In such an environment, no one would make up the notion that the women were the first (and primary) witnesses to the death and the entombment and then the empty tomb and the risen Jesus. This is a story no one would make up in Jesus' world if he or she wanted it to be believed by Jewish males— and other males as well. It is thus remarkable and surprising when we hear about Jesus having a whole coterie of female followers, not merely women in the villages, but also women who traveled with him. Luke 8:1-3 reads as follows:

> Soon afterward, Jesus traveled through the cities and villages preaching and proclaiming the good news of God's kingdom. The Twelve were with him, along with some women who had been healed of evil spirits and sicknesses. Among them were Mary Magdalene (from whom seven demons had been thrown out), Joanna (the wife of Herod's servant Chuza), Susanna, and many others who provided for them out of their resources. (CEB)

Several things are striking about this passage. If you examine all the references to women disciples in the Gospels, you will discover that Mary Magdalene is always mentioned first, except on one occasion, and the exception proves the rule. In John 20 we hear about Jesus' mother, and she and family members are mentioned before Mary Magdalene at the cross; but this is the only occasion we find such an ordering of the list of women. Otherwise, Mary Magdalene is mentioned first, just as Peter is mentioned first regularly among the Twelve. This suggests she is the leader of the female disciples. The second thing to be said about her is that her name is Miryam of Migdal. Magdalene is not her last name; it is just an Anglicized form of the village named Migdal, a small fishing village on the northwest corner of the Sea of Galilee.

Next, we must note that what we hear immediately about this woman is that she is a person from whom Jesus had cast seven demons. Now seven, in early Judaism, was the number of completion; or in this case it was a way of saying she was extremely possessed. She had dabbled with darkness and had paid the price of the powers of darkness taking over her life. We do not know if this happened through her consulting spirits as a medium or dealing with some form of witchcraft; but in any case, Jesus had set her free, and she in turn had dedicated herself to following and serving Jesus. More we cannot say on this subject. This woman was clearly not Jesus' wife at this juncture or later. You will notice that she addresses him as "my teacher" in John 20 when she sees him on Easter morning and grabs him. She does not address him as "my husband" (nor does she say, "I'm so glad you're back, honey! Let's jump-start our marriage again by reading a James Dobson book").[2] Furthermore, this Miryam is not the same person as either the anonymous sinner woman mentioned in Luke 7:36-50 or the anonymous woman caught in adultery mentioned in John 7:53–8:11. Both of these other women are sexually immoral women; but no such thing is said of Miryam, who is always mentioned by name. Her problem was spiritual, not sexual.

We are told in Luke 8:3 that Miryam and these other women were providing for Jesus and the Twelve out of their own means, but we should by no means conclude from this that they are being portrayed here simply as the traveling hospitality brigade. They too were Jesus' disciples, and Luke goes out of his way in Luke 23–24 to make clear that these very same named Galilean women are the women at the cross and the tomb, and are the ones who first receive the news at the empty tomb that Jesus has risen. Clearly, he portrays them as disciples who "remember" what Jesus had earlier taught them about his coming demise and draw the correct conclusions when they find the empty tomb.

We must imagine these women overcoming considerable obstacles and objections to be Jesus' traveling followers. For example, there were Jewish traditions that suggested that Jewish men should not talk or travel with women they were not closely related to or did not know well from their own village. Jesus was from Nazareth, and none of these women seem to have been from there. And furthermore, no member of Jesus' own family traveled with him as a sort of buffer either. We are told in John 7:5 that even Jesus' brothers did not believe in him during his ministry (for more, see pages 52-54). It would appear likely that Jesus set the tongues in Galilee wagging not only by having women disciples, but also by allowing them to go on the road with him when they were not kin to him. This was scandalous—as scandalous as Jesus dining with sinners and tax collectors and allowing sinful women to let down their hair and anoint his feet with oil.

The second named woman in the list in Luke 8:1-3 is Joanna, the wife of Chuza, Herod's estate agent. This is a high-status woman, no mere fishmonger's wife. One can only imagine that Chuza would have found his wife's behavior unacceptable. Indeed, in view of Herod Antipas's understanding of John and Jesus as popular itinerant Galilean prophetic figures that endangered his authority in Galilee, we can imagine Antipas telling Chuza to get his wife under control and not allow her to go walkabout with Jesus. This would be seen as a disgrace to Chuza, and in due course, if it didn't stop, Chuza would have had to choose between his job and a wife who was publicly shaming and humiliating him in the eyes of his employer. Imagine how Chuza felt when Joanna refused to stop following Jesus and indeed went all the way to Jerusalem with Jesus and this band of female disciples for the Passover. She was not just a sometime casual participant in Jesus' ministry. She was fully committed. And here is where the story of Joanna really gets interesting.

What happened to these women who traveled with Jesus from Galilee to Jerusalem at the end of his ministry, who witnessed his death, the empty tomb, the angels, and the risen Lord? We have one small but important clue in Acts 1:14 where we hear that they are in the upper room after Easter, praying in preparation for the sending of the Spirit, along with Mary, Jesus' mother, and some of his brothers. It appears that members of the holy family have finally come around to being followers of Jesus, like these women and the Twelve.

If we take a moment to read a short passage from a letter Paul penned in about A.D 57 to the church in Rome, we hear the following in Romans 16:7: "Greet Andronicus and Junia, my relatives who were in prison with me; they are prominent among the apostles, and they were in Christ before I was." The first thing to note about this little greeting is that Junia is the Latin form of the

Hebrew name Joanna. These two names are one and the same. The second thing to note is that Paul says this woman is a Jew, as is Andronicus (who is probably her husband). The third thing of interest is that Paul says she was in Christ—that is, became a Christian—before Paul did. Among other things, this means that she became a Christian in the first couple of years or so after Easter or even right at the beginning of the Easter events. Next we are told that Paul works with this couple; they are his coworkers. We know this because they had been imprisoned along with him somewhere and at some juncture. It was rare for women to be imprisoned at all, so they must have been involved in the work of public proclamation and someone felt they were a total nuisance. Last, and most important, Paul says they are noteworthy apostles, by which Paul means something quite specific. First Corinthians 9:1-2 lists that one of the qualifications for being an apostle in the Pauline sense was that one had to have seen the risen Lord. Andronicus and Junia are not merely missionaries from a local church, say at Antioch; they are apostles of the Lord—indeed, famous apostles from the outset of the Christian movement.

When you put all of this interesting information together, it is possible, indeed I would say probable, that this Junia (her Latin name is given here because Paul is writing to the Roman church where Latin is the primary language of the city) is one and the same as Joanna. What had happened is that Chuza had probably given her a writ of divorce since she would not give up following Jesus and she had later remarried someone in the movement, a fellow Christian who also had seen the risen Lord, one Andronicus. Now, more than twenty-five years later, they were apostles at work in Rome and still coworkers of Paul in the Christian ministry.

It would be nice if we knew a good deal more about Susanna and the other women who are not given names in Luke 8:1-3, but that text is sufficient to show that from the outset of Jesus' Galilean ministry, Jesus recruited female followers, and they proved to be some of the most reliable and trustworthy and loyal witnesses he ever had.[3] There is, however, another group of disciples that gets far too little press—the Judean disciples of Jesus, and, in particular, the family of Mary, Martha, and Lazarus.

THE BELOVED DISCIPLE AND HIS SISTERS

Even if we had only Luke 10:38-42, we would certainly know that Jesus had followers in and around Jerusalem. His was not just a Galilean ministry; and as the Fourth Gospel informs us, Jesus made repeated trips up to Jerusalem during his ministry, mostly, it would appear, at festival time. And there was a family he stayed with when he got close to Jerusalem, the family of Mary, Martha, and Lazarus in Bethany, on the southeastern corner of the city of Jerusalem.

We need to talk a bit about Jesus' Judean followers, and particularly the aforementioned family.

First it should be said that it is possible that there were Judeans among the Twelve. Judas Iscariot, for example, is a possibility, and also Simon the zealot. The reason I make these suggestions is because zealotic activity quite naturally tended to focus on the spiritual epicenter of Judaism, Jerusalem, and in Judea in general because it had become a Roman province with a Roman governor. We will see in a subsequent study that some of the disciples, on that fateful evening when Jesus was betrayed, thought they needed swords to fight the authorities if they tried to take Jesus captive.

More clearly, there is the family of Mary, Martha, and Lazarus. What do we know about this family? The story is something of a detective story, and it is worth spinning out at some length. Let's first notice that the term *Beloved Disciple* is nowhere mentioned in the Synoptic Gospels. Not a single disciple, including not one of the Twelve, is called this in Matthew, Mark, or Luke. It is a term applied to a disciple only in the Fourth Gospel, but to whom? Traditionally, many church fathers thought it referred to John, son of Zebedee. Other church fathers, however, realized that identification was very problematic.

For one thing, all of the special Zebedee traditions we find in Matthew, Mark, and Luke are entirely absent from the Gospel of John: the calling of the Zebedee brothers; their presence at the raising of Jairus's daughter; their presence at the Transfiguration of Jesus; their request for box seats when Jesus came into his dominion for good. None of these stories, which particularly involved the Zebedees, are mentioned in John, and this is passing strange if John Zebedee wrote this Gospel, since John 19–21 emphasizes that this Gospel is the testimony of an eyewitness and his unique experiences.

Second, we have to note that none of the Galilean miracles reported in the Synoptic Gospels recur in the Fourth Gospel, with only one exception—the feeding of the five thousand and the walking on water tandem. Otherwise, all the miracle tales in John are Judean miracles, or in the case of the Cana miracle, miracles that occurred in Galilee but are absent from the reporting in these earlier Gospels. Again, this is strange if the author of the Gospel of John is from Galilee. Then, too, there are further drastic differences in the portrayal of Jesus. There are no exorcisms by Jesus or his disciples in John, and basically there are no parables in John either, unless one counts something like the story of the vine and branches as a parable. Jesus' whole style of public discourse in the Fourth Gospel is different—involving "I am" sayings and long discourses linked to those seven "I am" sayings (e.g., "I am the bread of life," linked to the feeding of the five thousand). In addition, we hear in detail about Jesus' ministry in Samaria in John 4 and his encounter with Judean Jewish teachers like Nicodemus (John 3). In short, this Gospel is composed mostly of some very different stories from what we find in the Synoptics, and most of them have a Judean provenance. It follows from this that the author of this material is likely a Judean as well.

Third, we need to bear in mind that in the earliest period in Christian history, Christian house churches did not have multiple Gospels to compare to one another. Different Gospels served different regions of the church—Mark in Rome, Matthew in Galilee or Syria, Luke in Antioch or Greece, and John in Ephesus in modern-day Turkey. There was not a collection of the fourfold

Gospels until early in the second century, it would appear, and that is when they acquired the distinguishing labels "according to X, according to Y" and so on, so that one could be differentiated from another. Although the comparing of some Gospel accounts clearly has begun by the time Luke writes his preface in Luke 1:1-4, Luke does not know the accounts in the Fourth Gospel; but he certainly does know about the Zebedees.

Fourth, the sons of Zebedee are only mentioned once by that term in the Fourth Gospel—only in the appendix in John 21:2. No one hearing the Gospel of John for the first time would have guessed that someone only mentioned in passing in the appendix might be the author of this Gospel, might be the Beloved Disciple. Indeed, if they were hearing this Gospel afresh from the beginning, they would think through the story in the order in which it is presented and associate the term *Beloved Disciple* with someone else entirely.

For the first time, in John 11:1-3 we hear about "the one whom Jesus loved," and he is named *Lazarus*. It cannot be an accident that only after this juncture do we begin to have the phrase "the Beloved Disciple" in John 13 and following. Having introduced this language in John 11:1-3, the author of this material then proceeds to use it further thereafter. When we begin to put together the pieces of the puzzle, this makes so much better sense of the Johannine data than the suggestion that John Zebedee was the Beloved Disciple. It makes better sense of church history as well, because James Zebedee was martyred in the 40s, according to Acts 1–4, and it appears John may have been as well.[4] Whoever wrote the Fourth Gospel lived a very long and full life well into the first century A.D, as the end of John 21 makes perfectly clear. Let's review a few facts.

In the earliest record of a visit by Jesus to Bethany, we hear about his time in the house of Mary and Martha in Luke 10:38-42. There is something very odd about this story. It begins, "Now as they [Jesus and the disciples] went on their way, he [Jesus] entered a certain village, where a woman named Martha welcomed him into her home." Why did only Jesus go into this house? And while we are at it, why are these two sisters living together? Why aren't they married, considering they are adults? This is passing strange in regard to both these facts until we real-ize something important. It is Mary, Mary of Bethany, who will anoint Jesus' feet in gratitude for what he has done for her brother Lazarus, according to John 12, in the fullest account of the inci-dent. But we have a parallel account in Mark 14:3-9. If one ana-lyzes the two stories together, it is clearly the same story told in two slightly different ways. In John this transpires in the house of Mary and Martha, and in Mark 14 this house is called the house of Simon the leper. And now we are getting somewhere.

If Simon, the father of these three children, had died of lep-rosy, it is not a surprise that his adult son and daughters had not married. They would have been suspected of carrying the conta-gion. And indeed, for all we know, Lazarus himself may have died of Hansen's disease (leprosy). All the more reason the disciples might have initially stayed away from this house—that is, until Jesus had raised and healed Lazarus.

More important, let us consider a few pertinent facts, supposing the Beloved Disciple was in fact Lazarus. This then makes perfect sense of the scene at the cross in John 19, where we find Mary and the Beloved Disciple (hereafter BD). The former is bequeathed to the latter, and then the BD is said to have taken her into his own home. This home is not way up north in Galilee; it is in Bethany, a suburb of Jerusalem, which then explains why in Acts 1:14 we still find Mary in Jerusalem after Easter—she never left. It also comports with the Synoptic accounts, which inform us that all of the Twelve had abandoned Jesus and were not present at the Crucifixion. This does not contradict the Johannine presentation if the Beloved Disciple isn't one of the Twelve.

Or think again about the meal discussed in John 13. Jesus is reclining on the couch with the BD (v. 23), and we know that normal protocol was for the host to recline with the chief guest. Having just read in John 12 about the meal at Lazarus's house, there is no reason to think the meal in John 13 takes place any-where else; and there is good reason to think this is a different meal from the Last Supper, which happened on Thursday night of festival week. This meal in John 13 is said to have transpired several days before the festival of the Passover, not just one day before. This view of John 13 also explains why this story includes a dramatic foot washing of Peter and others, an event nowhere recorded in the Synoptics as part of the Passover celebration of Jesus with his disciples. That's because it happened at a meal earlier in the week, at Lazarus's house.

Furthermore, this view about the BD explains John 21:23 perfectly. Why had there been a rumor that the BD would not die before Jesus returned? Simple—Jesus had already raised Lazarus from the dead once and so some figured he would live until Jesus returned to earth. Or consider what is said in John 18:15. The BD (also called "the other disciple," a very odd title if it means another one of the Twelve but which makes perfect sense if it is referring to the leader of the Judean disciples, Lazarus, in other words, Peter's Judean counterpart) has an all-access pass into the house of Caiphas and the high priest is said to know him. This makes sense if Lazarus lives in the vicinity of Jerusalem, and in fact various elders of the community in Jerusalem, including some priests, visit his family during the weeklong mourning period (see John 11:31; "the Jews" refers to the "Jewish officials"). Or consider the fact that the BD knows where the new rock-cut tomb of Joseph of Arimathea is and beats Peter to the tomb when the women report it is empty on Easter morning. In short, the thesis that the Beloved Disciple is Lazarus fits all the facts and explains various conundrums in the Fourth Gospel.

Let's go back now and think about Lazarus's sisters, Mary and Martha. Just as Jesus had a home base in Galilee, in Capernaum, in the house of the chief disciple Peter's in-laws, so he had a home base in and around Jerusalem in the Bethany home of his chief Jerusalem disciples, the family of Lazarus. This in part explains why Jesus would go and visit these women alone. Let us also consider the term "the one whom Jesus loved" in more detail. At a minimum, this implies an ongoing relationship of some duration. Jesus hadn't merely had a nodding acquaintance with this family; in fact he was especially fond of them, visited them regularly, and ate with them. And the sisters could see perfectly clearly how much Jesus loved Lazarus. This is why the

emergency cry went out for Jesus to hasten to Bethany and inter-
vene on behalf of this beloved friend.

It is an interesting fact that the characterization of Martha and
Mary is remarkably similar in Luke 10:38-42 and in John 11–12.
Martha is the more vocal and outgoing one, and Luke implies she
must be the elder sister, as Martha is said to have hosted the din-
ner in Luke 10 at her house. Furthermore, we see the forward
nature of Martha not only in her complaining to Jesus that Mary
should come help in the kitchen, but also in John 11 where she
is first out the door to go and complain to Jesus that if only he
had been present he could have prevented Lazarus from dying.
Mary, by contrast, is more contemplative, more of a spiritual disciple. Notice in Luke 10 how she is portrayed as assuming the
posture of a disciple, sitting at the Master's feet and soaking up his
teaching. Notice as well how Jesus tells Martha that Mary has
chosen the good portion, the better food, and it will not be taken
from her so that she can help in the kitchen! Even for women,
Jesus set up the priority of being a disciple first and the hospitality brigade thereafter. And of course it is Mary in John 12 who
anoints Jesus in gratitude, an act Jesus reinterprets as a noble
preparation for his forthcoming death and burial. Finally, at the
tomb of Lazarus, it is Martha who does not understand what Jesus
means by saying he is the resurrection (and thus can raise Lazarus
on the spot) and laments that there will be a bad smell if Lazarus's
tomb is opened. Mary makes no such complaint.

Here then in Luke 10 and John 11–12 we have cameo portraits
of an important Judean family that were all disciples of Jesus and
provided support for his ministry when he was in town. It is not
surprising then that we have only in the Fourth Gospel
Jerusalem-based stories like the healing of the man born blind
(John 9), or the healing of the man by the pool of Bethesda in
Jerusalem (John 5), or even the miracle at Cana, which Jesus'
mother could have related to Lazarus when she stayed in his
home after the Crucifixion. Jesus' ministry in Judea took on a different character to that which he had in Galilee—different
teachings, different miracles, and even some different disciples.

We may be thankful we have at least one Gospel that focuses more on his Judean ministry.

So who wrote the Gospel of John? If we look at the very end of this Gospel, in John 21, we hear that this Gospel preserves the traditions of the Beloved Disciple, which he even wrote down, and then we hear, "And we know that his testimony is true." Who is the "we"? The "we" is the community of the Beloved Disciple. After the BD died, someone gathered his traditions together, edited them, and put them together in the form we now have. This person was a final editor, not an author, for the Beloved Disciple authored the materials in this Gospel. I would suggest he was John of Patmos, famous for authoring the book of Revelation and likely a member of the church in Ephesus (see Revelation 2–3—he writes to them first). This is why the Gospel, once it became public, came to be called "according to John." It was known that John had put it together. But John was not the Beloved Disciple; he was simply the literate prophet, in the community of the Beloved Disciple, who gave us this wonderful collection of the Beloved Disciple's memoirs, just as Mark gave us Peter's memoirs in his Gospel. It is understandable, of course, how many decades later this John, the seer of Patmos, might be confused with John Zebedee.[5]

A FAMILY AFFAIR—THE PHYSICAL FAMILY AND THE FAMILY OF FAITH

One of the things that seems to have most characterized the teaching and ministry of Jesus is his stress on the cost of discipleship. Seldom, however, do people stop to ponder what it may have cost Jesus' own family and what sort of relationship he may have had with them as a result of his ministry. Let us consider the facts.

By the time Jesus comes home to Nazareth to preach in the synagogue there, he has already been in ministry in Israel for some time, has built up a reputation, and indeed has become quite controversial. We will say much more about the story in

Luke 4 and Mark 6 in the next chapter, but we speak of it here in order to say something about the notable absence of Joseph on that occasion. In fact, after Luke 2:41-52, a story that takes place when Jesus was about twelve, in A.D 10 or so, we hear no more about Joseph in any of the Gospel texts that recount the ongoing ministry of Jesus. It seems clear enough that by the time Jesus begins his ministry in Galilee, Joseph has already passed away. Notice how Jesus is called "son of Mary" in Mark 6, which, besides being odd and pejorative language, seems to reflect the family state of affairs. This brings up a crucial point.

In the highly patriarchal world of Jesus, when a husband died prematurely and there were male heirs who were not yet married and did not have homes and lives of their own, it was the duty of the eldest son to "honor his father and mother" by becoming the head of the family and usually take over the family business. We know that Jesus was in fact a practitioner of the family business, for he himself is called a *tekton* (Mark 6:3), which means an artisan, someone who works in wood or stone.

Jesus is known in his hometown as one who has practiced the family trade. But he abandons this when he begins his ministry, so the duty of running the family business would then fall to the next eldest son. Since James is always listed first in the naming of Jesus' siblings (see Mark 6:3 and parallels), it seems clear he is the next eldest. Mary, in fact, had four boys and three girls after Jesus, and so we are talking about a lot of mouths to feed. One can immediately see that the ministry of Jesus could have been resented by James and the other siblings, if not rejected. They may have felt like the other townsfolk that Jesus was getting too big for his britches, and furthermore, Jesus had left them holding the bag of supporting the family.

This way of reading the evidence then explains why John 7:5 says the brothers did not (yet) believe in Jesus, even late in the ministry, and it in part explains why Jesus bequeaths his mother to the BD, not to his brothers, with his dying breath on the cross. Why would he do such a thing? The main reason is explained in a text like Mark 3:31-35. What with the eschatological saving activity of God breaking into human history through Jesus, he hardly had time to be a family man, either with his birth family or by marrying and having a family of his own. More to the point, for him the primary family was the family of faith, not the physical family, and indeed this explains sharp and pointed sayings like, "Don't think that I've come to bring peace to the earth. I haven't come to bring peace but a sword. For I've come to turn a man against his father, a daughter against her mother, a daughter-in-law against her mother-in-law. People's enemies are members of their own households" (Matt 10:34-36 CEB). It also helps explain the lament, "A prophet is not without honor, except in his hometown and among his relatives and in his own household" (Mark 6:4 ESV). Jesus was even misunderstood by his own family. "He came unto his own, and his own received him not," says John 1:11 (KJV). In terms of priorities then, the family of faith—whoever did the will of God—was to be his primary family. This explains the distancing, the misunderstanding, and even the failure to believe in Jesus by members of his family. Some of them seem to have thought Jesus had shamed and abandoned his family. Notice that none of Jesus' family are there at the cross, except his mother, and Jesus does not bequeath her back to the siblings.

This is a story that is dark, and in various ways, sad, before Easter. And indeed without Easter, there would never have been a happy ending for either the disciples or the physical family; there would never have been a rapprochement, a reconciliation, an understanding. In our next chapter we must focus some more on Jesus' ministry by the Sea of Galilee and on his teaching and healings that lead up to the climactic confrontation in the synagogue in Nazareth. When the Annunciation had come to that young girl Mary in Nazareth, she could never have imagined all the twists and turns in her story and that of her eldest son and all the heartache involved (see the warning in Luke 2:35: "And a sword will pierce your own soul too") leading up to the Announcement to the hometown folk.

A close reading of Mark 3:31-35 will reveal that Jesus refused to go home with his mother and siblings and instead said that his real family at that juncture was whoever did the will of God. It would appear that Mark 3:21 indicates one of the reasons he refused. They seem to have thought he was "beside himself," not in his right mind, presumably because of the exorcisms. Their assumption seems to have been that if you dance with the devil you're bound to get burned. They really did not understand; indeed, they were deeply troubled by the turn that Jesus' ministry had taken. But to further understand that ministry you need to understand what sort of wise man and prophet Jesus really was, to which we turn in the next chapter.

NOTES

1. There are of course later traditions about Thomas and other members of the Twelve going to far-flung places. For example, Thomas is said to have gone to India. These traditions may or may not have historical substance, but in any case, they do not reflect the activities of the Twelve as a unit. They reflect the fact that some of the Twelve, at least, took the Great Commission in Matthew 28 quite seriously.

2. On the whole issue of the relationship of Mary Magdalene to Jesus in the much later and unhistorical Gnostic Gospels of Philip and the Gospel of Mary, see Witherington, *The Gospel Code* (Downers Grove, Ill.: InterVarsity Press, 2004).

3. See Witherington, *Women and the Genesis of Christianity* (New York: Cambridge University Press, 1990), and also Eldon Jay Epp, *Junia: The First Woman Apostle* (Minneapolis: Fortress Press, 2005).

4. See Witherington, *What Have They Done with Jesus?* (San Francisco: HarperSanFrancisco, 2006).

5. See now Richard Bauckham's wonderful book on how the early church father Papias helps us understand all this—*Jesus and the Eyewitnesses* (Grand Rapids: William B. Eerdmans, 2006) and my *What Have They Done with Jesus?*

CHAPTER FOUR

FROM THE SEA TO THE WEDDING TO HOME

*Jesus was the reality of which Caesar and his sycophant
client kings were the parody.*

—N. T. Wright

THE JESUS BOAT AND SOME SEA SAGAS

The Sea of Galilee is really misnamed. It should be called a lake. You won't see any cruise ships on this lake, either. You will, however, find imitation Jesus boats. Perhaps you have heard the story about the great discovery in the mud near Capernaum, when the lake was low, of a first-century fishing boat. This boat is pretty amazing, not least because twelve different kinds of wood were used to make it. There could hardly be a more homemade boat. And though there is no inscription on the back of this boat that says, "Jesus slept here," it nonetheless gives us a good and vivid illustration of what the fishing boats of his era looked like. This one is indeed big enough to fit Jesus and the Twelve in it, all scrunched together, and you begin to get a mental picture of life on the Sea of Galilee, or Kinnert, or Tiberias—this lake went by all three names.

As precious and as important as water was to Jews of this era, it is interesting the sorts of theological ideas some Jews had about large bodies of water. Jews, unlike Phoenicians (a seagoing people), were landlubbers. They associated large bodies of water with danger, drowning, and chaos. In fact, in the Psalms drowning is the image the psalmist uses to describe a near-death experience from which God rescued him (see Ps 18:4-5, 16). Jews associated large bodies of water with sea monsters, like Leviathan (see Job 41; Ps 74, 104). And in the New Testament era, large bodies of water were thought to be the abode of ghosts and demons as well. This helps us understand several stories about Jesus' ministry in and around the Sea of Galilee.

Take, for example, the famous story where the disciples are rowing away through heavy wind, trying to get to shore (Mark 6:45-51), and Jesus walks on water toward them. They are terrified, thinking it is a ghost churned up by the undulating waters. Or think for a moment of the famous story of the Gerasene demoniac (Mark 5), or as one preacher called it, the story of "deviled ham." Jesus has gone across the lake to the Golan Heights, where there are Gentiles. There are also herds of pigs, something you would not find in Israel. Jesus must deal with a legion of demons in a poor man who has been cast out from his village and lives in a graveyard, a place of uncleanness from a Jewish point of view. In the process of being exorcized, the demons request to be cast into the pigs. From a Jewish point of view, this is completely logical—unclean spirits being put into unclean animals. And then they run pell-mell into the chaotic waters—perfect! This story would have produced some wry smiles in its day.

Then of course there is the famous story of Jesus asleep at the wheel, or, in this case, in the stern of the boat (Mark 4). A storm comes up, churning up the sea, and the disciples come unglued. Jesus is awakened and stills both the wind and the sea. The Sea of Galilee sits in a depression surrounded by hills, creating a sort of natural bowl, and swirling winds can come and go in this vortex quite quickly. But once a sea is churned up, it normally stays choppy, and these veteran fishermen are stunned that the sea suddenly is completely placid. It raises the proper question: "Who then is this, that even the wind and the sea obey him?" In the Jewish way of thinking, only God could control the chaotic waters.

In three straight chapters (Mark 4–6), Mark tells us tales about Jesus' adventures on or near the Sea of Galilee—adventures that even impressed those who had spent their life on this body of water and made their living from it. In fact, in the first six or so chapters of Mark, Jesus seems to be regularly going back and forth across the sea of Galilee, preaching, teaching, and healing as he goes. And not incidentally, he shows no fear of water, and even uses walking on water as a test of faith for one like Simon, who had grown up with a healthy fear and respect of water and the Jewish views of it. In Mark Twain's delightful account of his own tour of the Holy Land in *The Innocents Abroad*, he tells of the day he came to the Sea of Galilee, looking for a ride on it. An Arab boatman offered to give him such a ride—for fifty dollars (an enormous sum in the late nineteenth century). In response to this exorbitant offer, Twain quipped, "I now see why Jesus chose to walk on water!"

If one looks carefully, one can indeed see that so many of the early stories of Jesus are connected to water, and this is in part because they are set in Galilee and by the Jordan. Whether we think of the baptism of Jesus, these stories just mentioned, or the story of Jesus and the Samaritan woman (John 4) where Jesus declares that he himself is the living water (a phrase that normally means "running water"), water figures prominently in these tales. In Judea this is less the case, except for the Pool of Bethesda tale. Jesus' mastery over water, in water, on water, and with water is meant to tell us much about who he is in a land where fresh water is the most vital, prized commodity of all.

Humans can live a long time, many days indeed, without solid food, as long as they have clean water. In one of the most ancient churches in all of Jordan, in a little place called Medaba, there is a mosaic map in the most ancient part of the floor of that church. One of the most interesting features of the map is the picture of the Jordan flowing out of the Sea of Galilee and into the Dead Sea. In the picture, fish are swimming down the Jordan—that is, until they get to the Dead Sea, and there they are depicted as being smart enough to do a U-turn. The Salt, or Dead, Sea could sustain no life and stood in complete contrast to the Sea of Galilee, which teemed with fish. These two contrasting seas were a clear and ever-present reminder to Jews in Galilee and elsewhere of how important water truly was, particularly fresh water.[1] But sometimes even good, clean water is not enough, even if it is water used for cleaning human beings, and this leads us to the famous story of the wedding feast at Cana, told in John 2.

JESUS—THE LIFE-GIVING ONE AT THE WEDDING PARTY

The story of the wedding feast at Cana is much beloved but also much belabored. For our purposes, it is a story of interest because it gives us a glimpse of the period between the very beginning of Jesus' ministry and the debacle at Nazareth recorded in Luke 4 and Mark 6. At this point in time, Jesus has a few disciples, and he is still in touch with and in communion with his own family. In fact, the end of the story says that Jesus, his disciples, his mother, and his brothers all go down to Capernaum together, where they remain for a few days. At this point there is not a sharp or clear demarcation dividing the family of faith and Jesus' own family, and so this story is of historical as well as theological interest.

Few things in the Fourth Gospel lack symbolic and deeper meaning, if one can discern it, and we are directly told in John 2:11 that the miracle at the Cana wedding was the first of the "signs" that Jesus performed, revealing who he was to at least those who noticed and had eyes to see. What is interesting about Jesus' miracles is that he never performs them to "wow" the crowds. You cannot impress people into the dominion of God anyway, and Jesus was well aware of this. Even a nature miracle like that recorded in John 2 is an act of compassion, not an attempt to prove to anyone who Jesus is. And in fact only Jesus' mother and a few disciples, and perhaps the servants manning the purification jars, really even knew a miracle had transpired on this occasion.

One of the larger themes in the sign narratives in the first half of the Gospel of John is that Jesus replaces the festivals and institutions of Judaism with himself. He is the Lamb of God; his body is the temple where God dwells; he is the Bread of Life and the Living Water; and he (rather than Israel) is the true or authentic vine, and so on. This story further beats the drum on that note, for here Jesus replaces the old Jewish purification water with the new—and best—wine of the Gospel. Lifeless water becomes gallons of Gallo in the Master's hands. Of course, some have disputed whether Jesus really created an alcoholic beverage here, and in fact the joke about my own denomination (the United Methodists) is that while Jesus turned water into wine, the Methodists have attempted to change it back into water ever since! Be that as it may, wine in Jesus' world was certainly alcoholic, though perhaps not having as high an alcoholic content as some modern fortified wines. One of the proofs that the story in John 2 is dealing with more than grape juice is the famous comment of the toastmaster: "You have, quite beyond the normal protocol, saved the best wine for last." The normal protocol was to serve the most alcoholic and flavorful wine first, while people still had discriminating palates, and then serve the B-class or watered-down wine. This was true at both Jewish and Greco-Roman banquets in that era. It is quite beyond the realm of the possible that a toastmaster at a Jewish wedding would have said, "You saved the best Welch's for last."

Another interesting feature about the Johannine sign miracles is that there is no description of *how* these miracles happen. It's not the process the Evangelist is interested in but rather the outcome. Water was changed into a huge quantity of wine—anywhere from 120 to 180 gallons of wine resulted from this miraculous transformation! Many of the miracles in the Fourth Gospel are of the stupendous quality (cf. for example the healing of the man born blind, an act nowhere recorded in the Old Testament, or the raising of a man four days dead—Lazarus). In fact it can be said there is a crescendo of the miraculous in John's Gospel. Nevertheless, the miracle at Cana is a stupendous one, to say the least.

Of particular interest for our purposes is the interchange between Jesus and his mother. There are in fact two interchanges between Jesus and his mother, and they bookend this Gospel's portrayal of the ministry of Jesus—one here at Cana at the outset and one at the cross. In both places Jesus does not call Mary his mother. Rather, he uses the distancing language of "woman," which may seem odd to us, except that it makes clear Jesus could not act on his earthly mother's authority and say so; he had to act on the authority of his heavenly Father, and he waits for that go-ahead at various junctures in these Johannine stories (see for example John 11:1-4). The second thing to notice is that Cana is very close to Nazareth but, in fact, the family of Jesus goes down to Capernaum after this wedding—perhaps they were checking up on and checking out the ministry Jesus had already begun in that place.

On first blush, Jesus' mother comes across as pushy, and not too subtle, either. She says, "They have no [more] wine" (John 2:3). The celebration is winding down and the host, in this case the bridegroom, has run out of wine. Now, what we know about such first-century celebrations is that normally even in a small village like Cana there would be caterers who could supply more wine at the drop of a hat. Mary's implicit request then seems a bit out of the ordinary, unless of course she felt some obligation to help. Perhaps, since this village is very near to Nazareth, we are talking about the wedding of one of Jesus' relatives.

In any case, Jesus' response seems brusque: "Woman, what concern is that to you and to me? My hour has not yet come" (John 2:4). There is much in this little exchange. Is Jesus suggesting that he and his mother have no obligation in this situation? That is possible. But the phrase "my hour" may suggest that while Mary may have felt obligated, Jesus did not. But this raises the question about what Jesus means by "my hour." If we survey this Gospel, it seems clear that what he means is that it is not yet time for him to reveal himself to the world. He's on a timetable set by the Father, not his mother, and he must await the appointed hour, the propitious time to fully reveal his identity. Ironically, this turns out to be the hour of his death—real prime time. Jesus' identity is most and best revealed not in his miracles, but when he has "his hour" on the cross.

Mary doesn't haggle with Jesus; she simply assumes that good-hearted Jesus will do something without violating his own eschatological clock. So she says to the servants, "Do whatever he tells you" (John 2:5). The ball is left in Jesus' court, and it seems to be presumed that he can figure out a way to help without making a public spectacle or issue of himself through a miracle. As it turns out, even the shocked toastmaster doesn't know where this vintage wine came from, nor could he have suspected it was instantaneously created by the one who brings the new wine of the Gospel. And so the story says that however quietly, indirectly, and to however few people, "Jesus did this, the first of his signs, in Cana of Galilee, and revealed his glory; and his disciples believed in him" (John 2:11). Of course, the story implies that Mary already had taken the measure of her Son and knew he could do miracles.

In the Fourth Gospel a faith in someone as a miracle worker, however positive it may be, is not the same thing as a faith in Jesus as the only begotten of God. The big picture in the Fourth Gospel, and what gives it so much irony, is that the hearer of this Gospel knows from the outset that Jesus is the incarnation of the Logos, the preexistent Son of God. But the characters in the narrative, including the disciples, do not know this, and in fact it does not dawn on any of the disciples until after Easter, when Jesus appears to Thomas and we finally have Jesus confessed as "my Lord and my God." Just as there is a crescendo of miracles in this Gospel, so there is also a crescendo of true confessions. If Jesus shows a certain disengagement from his mother's authority over him in this story, we see a reengagement at the cross when Mary is enfolded into the family of faith by Jesus' putting her into the safekeeping of the Beloved Disciple. The reference to "my hour" points us further to that only other episode involving Jesus and Mary—the encounter at the foot of the cross. God had indeed kept the best wine until last, in the person of his Son, and when the disciples got even a glimpse of his glory it made their hearts glad and nourished their faith in him. Although this story does not suggest Jesus was a party animal or that he was the life of the party in the usual sense of that term, he was indeed the one who brought life to the party through the vivifying act of changing water into wine. However, the joy of this moment contrasts starkly with the tone of the story we must now look at—the debacle over the sermon of Jesus in Nazareth.

THE ANNOUNCEMENT AT NAZARETH: THE REJECTION AT HOME

Thomas Wolfe, a great American novelist from my home state of North Carolina, wrote two novels with the word *home* in the title: *Look Homeward Angel* and *You Can't Go Home Again*. It is the latter title that would be the more apt description of what Jesus discovered when he went home to preach in the synagogue in Nazareth. In order to understand the context of that watershed event in Jesus' life, we need to explore a bit about daily life in Nazareth first.

Nazareth, like Bethlehem, was a one-stoplight town on no major road. In Jesus' day, you had to want to go to Nazareth to get there. Its one virtue, from an economic point of view, was that it happened to be very close to a whole new city that was being built by Herod Antipas—namely, Sepphoris, only three to four miles down one hill and up the next. Expense was not being spared in the building of Sepphoris. There were palatial mansions; there was to be a remarkable, large synagogue; there were all sorts of public and private structures going up as Herod decided he needed to try and outdo his father in public-works construction. This is of importance to us because undoubtedly it would have meant work—a lot of viable and valuable work—for the good citizens of Nazareth. Those who were skilled workers with their hands—stone carvers, carpenters, and others in related trades—would be in luck when this new boomtown began to be constructed during this very period before and when Jesus was beginning his ministry. It is indeed possible that Jesus himself, before he turned thirty and before John baptized him, had actually worked in Sepphoris, though we cannot be sure.

Of interest is a Greek word that Jesus used rather regularly to critique the Pharisees and others—*hypocrites*. We know the word transliterated into English as *hypocrite*. But in fact the original meaning of the word is "someone who acts in a play." What we know about Sepphoris is that it was a Hellenized Jewish city, a city where Greek culture and values were blended together or syncretized with Jewish culture and values. This sort of thing had of course been going on in the Holy Land for centuries—since the time of Alexander the Great—only now it was part Jewish–part Idumean rulers like Herod who were aping the building behavior of previous Hellenistic kings and overlords, attempting to raise their honor rating through public works. One of those public facilities in Sepphoris was a theater, where Jesus may well have heard about or learned a few Greek loan words, including the word *hypocrites*.

Daily life in Nazareth was simple. It does not appear they had a lot of wood for woodworking, but they had plenty of stone, and houses were made of stone. *Tektos* (from which we get the word *technical*) means someone who is an artisan who works with his hands, whether a carpenter or a stonemason. Maybe there was a reason Jesus and his followers talked about him as the stone the builders rejected—he may have been such a builder. More certainly, daily life would have involved these sorts of pursuits as well as agrarian work—picking and crushing olives, figs, grapes, and other fruit; growing grains, including wheat; planting vegetables and the like. Life revolved around the rainy season and the crop cycles, and for those very religious, the festivals, which one would journey up to Jerusalem to take part in.

It is a mistake to underestimate how pious and religious these Jews in Galilee were. One of the clearer and more remarkable archaeological discoveries in nearby Cana is a number of *mikvahs*, ritual purification baths; and we have springs and baths in Nazareth too. This is important because it shows that even small-town Jews were religiously observant, a fact shown even more clearly by there being a synagogue in Nazareth.

The synagogue in Nazareth would not have been as splendid and elaborate as the one in either Capernaum or Sepphoris. For one thing, it would not have had the royal bankroll paying for its building ("Your tax dollars at work"). Nazareth was a small village where everyone knew everyone else and knew everyone's business as well. This meant, without question, that the towns-folk in Nazareth knew something about the origins of Jesus, or assumed they did, as we shall see in a moment. Daily life would have moved along at a slow pace with normal mundane activities, except for the "ceasing" and worshiping and praying on Shabbat. And then something extraordinary happened one Shabbat in Nazareth, and we are still talking about it today.

Mark 6:1-6 says the following:

> Jesus left there and went to his hometown, accompanied by his disciples. When the Sabbath came, he began to teach in the synagogue, and many who heard him were amazed.
>
> "Where did this man get these things?" they asked. "What's this wisdom that has been given him, that he even does miracles! Isn't this the carpenter? Isn't this Mary's son and the brother of James, Joseph, Judas and Simon? Aren't his sisters here with us?" And they took offense at him.
>
> Jesus said to them, "Only in his hometown, among his relatives and in his own house is a prophet without honor." He could not do any miracles there, except lay his hands on a few sick people and heal them. And he was amazed at their lack of faith. (NIV)

The account is much more expansive in Luke 4:16-30, so we will quote it as well for comparison purposes:

> [Jesus] went to Nazareth, where he had been brought up, and on the Sabbath day he went into the synagogue, as was his custom. And he stood up to read. The scroll of the prophet Isaiah was handed to him. Unrolling it, he found the place where it is written:
>
> "The Spirit of the Lord is on me,
>   because he has anointed me
>   to preach good news to the poor.
> He has sent me to proclaim freedom for the prisoners
>   and recovery of sight for the blind,
> to release the oppressed,
>   to proclaim the year of the Lord's favor."
>
> Then he rolled up the scroll, gave it back to the attendant and sat down. The eyes of everyone in the synagogue were fas-

tened on him, and he began by saying to them, "Today this scripture is fulfilled in your hearing."

All spoke well of him and were amazed at the gracious words that came from his lips. "Isn't this Joseph's son?" they asked.

Jesus said to them, "Surely you will quote this proverb to me: 'Physician, heal yourself! Do here in your hometown what we have heard that you did in Capernaum.' "

"I tell you the truth," he continued, "no prophet is accepted in his hometown. I assure you that there were many widows in Israel in Elijah's time, when the sky was shut for three and a half years and there was a severe famine throughout the land. Yet Elijah was not sent to any of them, but to a widow in Zarephath in the region of Sidon. And there were many in Israel with leprosy in the time of Elisha the prophet, yet not one of them was cleansed—only Naaman the Syrian."

All the people in the synagogue were furious when they heard this. They got up, drove him out of the town, and took him to the brow of the hill on which the town was built, in order to throw him down the cliff. But he walked right through the crowd and went on his way. (NIV)

No matter how you slice it, neither of these renditions of the visit to Nazareth involves much of anything good. In both, the hometown folk clearly reject Jesus. In Luke it even goes so far as an attempt to stone Jesus, as the first step in the process of stoning was to throw someone off a hill or cliff; and then they would stone the person. Talk about being the stone that the builders rejected! Jesus was the stonemason who rejected a stoning and passed through the crowd somehow (we are not told how). Let's back up and see what led to this outcome and what it tells us about Jesus.

First of all, Luke tells us that it was Jesus' custom to go to the synagogue on the Sabbath. It also turns out to be his custom to say or do controversial things in the synagogue on the Sabbath, including nonemergency healings. Second, we need to bear in mind that the synagogue was likely the one place in town, and the Sabbath the one time in the week, where and when the whole community, or most of it, would all come together. Instead of randomly fishing for followers, in a synagogue it was more like catching fish already in a barrel—that is, if they wanted to be caught. Third, notice that Jesus is literate—he can read the Scriptures (unlike the majority of the audience, it would appear)—and someone must have thought he was an appropriate person to speak in that synagogue or else the president of the synagogue or its ruler would not have allowed it in the first place. Perhaps it was a matter of curiosity. We cannot be sure.

The next thing to notice about this event is that Mark tells us the disciples came with Jesus and witnessed this debacle. It would doubtless be a story they would revisit time and again, because the one place a man expected to be most honored and accepted was in his hometown and at home. If he was shamed or rejected there, it was a shock; and notice that the Markan account begins and ends with the exclamation of amazement. At first, when Jesus taught, the crowd was amazed at his knowledge. In the end, Jesus was amazed at their unbelief in him and in things eschatological. This may be the one time where a Gospel writer really emphasizes that Jesus was surprised by something. He did not expect to be rejected or severely critiqued, much less nearly stoned, on this occasion.

If we read the Markan and Lukan accounts carefully, we will notice that in both cases there seems to have been an initially favorable response to Jesus' reading of the word and his brief commentary; but then the more the crowd began to think about who they thought Jesus was, the more they took umbrage to him and what he had to say. Notice as well that Jesus assumes the proper posture of a teacher—he reads the Scriptures and then he sits down, perhaps in the seat of Moses. Jesus of course mentions the existence of such a seat in the Gospels, and one has actually been found at the nearby synagogue in Korazin, a place Jesus also visited. In the synagogue, the teacher sits and the congregation stands. I tell my students it should still be that way.

Now let's talk briefly about what went on in a synagogue service. There would be prayers; there would be singing; there would probably be announcements; there would be a reading and exposition of Scripture; and there may well have been a time for questions and answers, or at least dialogue. It is the latter we see going on for most of this passage. We hear nothing in Mark, and precious little in

Luke, about Jesus' exposition of Isaiah 61—only that Jesus is implicitly claiming to be fulfilling that scripture through his ministry.

Isaiah 61 is an interesting text, and what is most interesting is not just which bits Jesus recites but the bit he omits—in particular, the second part of verse 2 that reads: "and the day of vengeance of our God." Jesus stops just short of this part of the oracle, and it suggests that his intent was to come to his hometown and proclaim good news—the good news of God's salvation, which he was bringing to one and all. But then there was the surprising, indeed scandalous, increasingly negative reaction to Jesus and the fact that he would dare to speak to them in an authoritative way. Jesus then turns, according to Luke, to a discussion of the judgment Nazareth would face for rejecting him. This was not a matter of personal pique or wounded pride, because he speaks elsewhere about the judgment that will fall on Capernaum and Korazin for having reacted negatively to his words and deeds.

The importance of Jesus' citing of Isaiah 61 and then claiming he was fulfilling it, can hardly be overstated. Jesus is implying that he is the one who fulfills the promises and prophecies of the Scriptures, such as this oracle. Furthermore, Isaiah 61 seems to be about the coming of a final eschatological day of Jubilee when debt slaves will be emancipated, the brokenhearted healed, the prisoners released, and the oppressed (presumably Jesus means the possessed) liberated. The Jewish notion that there would be a final, eschatological Jubilee, or freedom time, means that Jesus is in fact making the Emancipation Proclamation in his hometown. You may be saying: "What's the problem with that? Isn't that good news?"

The other side of this proclamation of course is the implicit suggestion that the hometown folk need to be liberated, need to be set free, need to be healed, and the like; and of course this requires that they admit they have such a need. Not only do they take umbrage to the idea that Jesus, who they saw grow up, might now be talking to them in this way; they don't like the spiritual implications about what it says about them, either. And the coup de grâce comes when they begin to start remembering and trotting out what they see as the mundane or perhaps even scandalous pedigree of Jesus.

In our earliest account of this event, in Mark, the response is "Where did this fellow get all this? What's the source of his wisdom on these matters? What mighty works has he done (here)?" And then we hear the insult: "Is this not the artisan, the son of Mary?" Now, in a patriarchal culture, even if a person's father had died, you did not call someone a son of his mother. This was clearly pejorative, more pejorative than calling him a momma's boy, and perhaps very little less pejorative than calling him an S.O.B. Even more pointedly, calling Jesus the son of Mary suggests someone thinks they know he was in fact an illegitimate child, a child born out of wedlock. In an honor-and-shame patriarchal culture, this was a way to talk about a person if you wanted to shame him or her.

Furthermore, they go on to suggest they know very well who Jesus really is because they know all his brothers and sisters, can name the lot, and none of them have been acting up or acting out like this. Jesus has four brothers and several sisters—it's a big Jewish family—and the implication is Jesus should not be putting on airs and pretending he is better than his blood kin, who are ordinary residents of Nazareth.

In Mark, Jesus responds by offering the famous "a prophet is not without honor except . . ." saying, which reminds us that Jesus did see himself as a prophet. Mark then rapidly rounds off the story by saying Jesus couldn't do much good there because of the unbelief in him, and we hear about Jesus' amazement at such unbelief. This must have been both a shocking and tremendously sad day for Jesus.

In Luke's account we hear more about the sequel to the teaching, and here we have Jesus calling himself a physician and suggesting it would be best if he cured himself first before critiquing Nazareth. The upshot of what follows is that Jesus intuits they are complaining that he hasn't done the healings at home that he had done elsewhere. Next we get the prophet saying found in Mark, and then Jesus has the courage or audacity to tell them that because of their unbelief even non-Jewish foreigners will get help and healing before them, as in the days of Elijah and Elisha, the other great northern prophets. This causes the congregation to fly into a rage and start the process of stoning.

On a superficial glance at things, it would appear that neither Jesus nor John had learned the ancient or modern art of sucking up to a crowd, including a hometown crowd, or could care less about using it if they knew it. In fact, Jesus had begun with gracious words about the good news and with nothing about the day of vengeance. But things went downhill thereafter when the crowd began to assess who they thought he was. One last thought about that. In Luke 4:22 someone says, "Is this not Joseph's son?" Of course the proper answer to that is no—they really don't know who Jesus really is, though they assume they do! It's presumption that guides their response.

Here ends the first phase of Jesus' Galilean ministry in dramatic, and also traumatic, fashion. We will not hear of Jesus trying to go home again; nor will we hear of Jesus interacting with his family again anytime soon. For Jesus, it was back to Capernaum or elsewhere, if he was to call anywhere home. As we will see in our second study, *On the Road with Jesus: Teaching and Healing*, the rising tide of opposition already evident in Nazareth was only going to increase in size and volume as time went on. There would even be death threats. Israel under client kings in Galilee and under direct Roman rule in Judea was volatile, even when it was not violent; and when someone came promising liberation but did not deliver the goods, in this case by not doing miracles at home, the response could be violent.

Jesus had not yet begun to talk about his eventual demise—but he would. In fact, it is not surprising that a person like Jesus, or like John, met a violent, premature death. Considering what Jesus said and did, and how controversial he was in various ways, I'm even surprised he lasted as long as he did, having something like a three-year ministry. We will say much more about this in our next study. Here I will leave you with a story.

I was born and raised in High Point, North Carolina, which was then, in 1951, well on the way to being the furniture capital of America. There were dozens of active furniture factories there. My father worked for one, and I had a summer job at another. Only a few years ago, I was invited back to my home church to preach and give a seminar, and help them celebrate an anniversary. I honestly did not know what to expect; but in my case I got a very different reception than Jesus did when he went home. I saw and hugged old friends, a favorite elementary schoolteacher, and old schoolmates; and I breathed in the air of the church where I first learned the cost of discipleship. In one sense, I could go home again. But in another sense, all had changed. There was only one working furniture factory still in town, and there was a sadness about the loss of that great industry and the loss of so many good jobs, all outsourced to China and elsewhere. It was bittersweet for me. I even visited High Point University, the college where I taught my first course on Jesus, in 1981. I could go home again, but alas, it was no longer home, even with a warm reception.

I imagine Jesus realized much more clearly than I did during my visit that his former home could not be his present one. Jesus was to go on to say, "Foxes have holes, and birds of the air have nests; but the Son of Man has nowhere to lay his head" (Matt 8:20; Luke 9:58). He became a holy vagabond, almost always on the road. It is a bad day when the hometown Messiah is forlorn, and foresworn by his own neighbors and kin. Indeed, in that sort of agrarian culture with tight-knit kin groups, to be shamed at home and cast out of one's town was a social disaster, not merely a sad event. One lost one's social network. It is a bad day when the man named Jesus of Nazareth is no longer welcome in Nazareth. Jesus knew the implications, and so he laid his hand to the plow and did not look back in longing. Instead, he looked forward, and what he saw on the horizon was the outline of a cross.

NOTE

1. An interesting side note is that you will remember the saying of Jesus about being the salt of the earth and salt losing its savor. Some commentators point out that salt can't lose its savor. This is not quite true if we are talking about impure salt, salt with various mineral additives, which you can find some of at the Dead Sea, even to this day. Jesus knew his surroundings very well, and he uses these realities to comment on things theological and spiritual.